Person-Centered/Client-Centered

Person-Centered/Client-Centered

Discovering the Self that One Truly Is

Doug Bower
Editor

iUniverse, Inc.
New York Lincoln Shanghai

Person-Centered/Client-Centered
Discovering the Self that One Truly Is

iUniverse, Inc.

For information address:
iUniverse, Inc.
2021 Pine Lake Road, Suite 100
Lincoln, NE 68512
www.iuniverse.com

All contributions have been used with the permission of the authors.

ISBN: 0-595-29530-4

Printed in the United States of America

Dedication

I dedicate this material to the late John Shlien, Ph.D. My first meeting with John was in a small group at the New York City meeting of the Association for the Advancement of the Person-Centered Approach. I watched in shock as he jumped on a presenter in the community meeting prior to our meeting. The shock was related to my mythology concerning unconditional positive regard. I have since drastically altered my position, no longer holding that positive regard is unconditional and that acceptance may not always be positive regard.

I found that John Shlien also questioned the accuracy of saying that acceptance was unconditional positive regard.

With subsequent meetings at annual workshops in Warm Springs, Georgia, our relationship grew. Our first small group experience was open, warm and cordial. Later encounters at Warm Springs were less so, but mutually respectful. I found in John a person who accepted my awkwardness with the person-centered approach without patronizing me in that acceptance. In one post I received from him in response to material I posted on a person-centered network, he told me that I was like a "bull in a china shop." I don't remember my words in response. I do remember wondering if the person-centered approach was so fragile that it could be compared to a china shop. I am sure that my response to him included this wonderment. I actually felt flattered by being called a bull.

John played a significant role in my joining that person-centered Internet network.

I found over the years that while John was not always warm, he was always encouraging. I suspect that played a role in my altering my position on acceptance.

Contents

Foreword

I keep pushing on the envelope of this approach feeling that the approach is too closely aligned with Carl Rogers. In this I get a variety of protests. On one end are those who say, "I am a Rogerian and proud of it." On the other end, there are those like my Internet colleague Tony Merry who claims that the term Rogerian hasn't been used for forty years and that there are a host of practitioners and scholars who are asserting the person-centered approach who are not calling themselves Rogerians.

Pete Sanders of PCCS Books in the United Kingdom has done a great deal towards opening the door for the scholars and practitioners to publish. He has published a myriad of titles and themes. My concerns are somewhat alleviated by his efforts.

Still, while Britain and Europe may not have the same affinity for Rogers as American scholars and practitioners have, I remain concerned that here in America the approach is too closely associated with and thus limited to Rogers's perspective of the approach.

Thus, my first project "The Person-Centered Approach: Applications for Living" was an attempt to apply the approach drawing in Rogerians and others not so tightly Rogerian into a project that offers the approach on a practical basis.

This project does even more so, though the focus is upon the theory related to the discovery of the self that one truly is.

I actually believe that, of all the theories in psychotherapy and education, the person-centered approach offers the quickest means of access to the self. The more confrontive and directive styles of other approaches have to cut through a host of defenses. I believe this in part due to the aggressive nature of confrontation and directiveness. Such approaches foster defensiveness. The person-centered approach does not stir that pot of the soul in the same manner and thus people open up faster and get at who they are. How does one become defensive with someone who is simply seeking to understand their perspective rather than seeking to change that perspective?

The contributors for this present project are approaching this theme of discovering the self in their own way. I am not even convinced that all the authors kept this theme in mind as they wrote. It certainly wasn't in the minds of those who had material that was written before this project was started and who contributed that material to enhance this effort.

I rather like that, as I often strive for not influencing people's perspectives. I would rather see their position free of my expectations. I feel very confident that this is the case with this project. I am also very confident that all the material contributes to this book's theme of discovering the self that one truly is.

Preface

This project is about the theory surrounding the liberating or discovering of one's self. I am simply offering perspectives from myself and others, which I believe open the door to discovery.

This effort is about three groups of people: 1) The writers who have something to write; 2) the readers who are interested in this topic and want to explore the work of these writers; and 3) anyone who seeks to discover one's self whether in therapy, education, or any other social setting.

Each chapter was reviewed. Some authors like myself needed more editing than others. However, the reviews and editing were not designed to coerce writers to conform to expectations through rewrites. Rather, they were designed to capture mistakes in grammar and syntax. Even then, it has been my experience that errors slip by the editors. Personally, I would rather not hide such awkwardness. Editing was also concerned with readability. That is, I am not interested in producing a project that only a handful of people can grasp. I am satisfied that all the contributions are readable and yet very thoughtful.

So, this project is about a genuine interaction between the authors and the readers. What you see is what you get.

I also believe that each chapter reflects work that the author believes captures the writer's satisfaction. That is, it says what the author wants to say rather than what an editor wants to say.

The reader can now decide if the material is worthwhile and satisfying. There is no effort from an editor predetermining or assuming that the material meets the reader's satisfaction, or even if it is good writing save for what was described above.

List of Contributors

Louis B. Fierman, M.D.: Associate Clinical Professor in Psychiatry, Yale University, New Haven, Connecticut

Graham Harris: writer, the Canary Islands

Jerry Krakowski: sociologist practicing in Westwood, CA

Grigoris Mouladoudis: Department of Primary Education, University of Ioannina, Greece

Alexandros Kosmopoulos: Department of Education, University of Patras, Greece

Mhairi MacMillan: counselor, supervisor and small group facilitator in Britain.

C. H. Patterson: Professor Emeritus, University of Illinois.

Introduction

In keeping with a personal philosophy holding that writers can express their own ideas and readers can interpret what they read, I have decided not to use an introduction to summarize the parts of this project. I generally feel I can't do justice to the writer, including my own writing by making such summaries. Further, I don't want to bias the reader by submitting my interpretations of the material.

Writers and readers have vast resources for engaging each other even if there is misunderstanding. I see no reason to impose my views as editor on the process of author/reader interaction. Writers are quite capable of deciding if their efforts say what they want them to say. The readers are quite capable of deciding whether they like the materials or not, or agree with them or not.

I am also excited to submit the project in the relatively new domain of "On-Demand Publishing." The final submissions took place via the Internet. This form of publishing has caught-on in the publishing domain for the time being. I like the risk involved. I like the freedom to publish with little to no interference from external committees or decision makers. The form is great for this project.

This is a wonderful time to publish and share ideas as the Internet touches peoples' lives bringing together new technology with a traditional paper format.

I now entrust this project to the readers. Hopefully, it will stimulate thoughts and perhaps be an encouragement to someone else to prepare a similar project.

The Self That One Truly Is

Doug Bower

I tend to believe that, whether the person-centered approach is only limited to therapy, or whether it is also applied to other settings, the approach is about participating in the discovery of the self that one truly is. This self is like snowflakes in that it has common characteristics, but each self is unique. Even "identical" twins have unique and separate selves.

It has been argued by some, (Brodley, 1999, Bozarth 1998, and Bower, 1985), that self-actualization is a foundation stone for the person-centered approach.

Personally, I have augmented my (1985) position and suspect that a person doesn't ever have to know of self-actualization in order to claim to be person-centered. However, I personally like the concept and seek here to present a snap shot of my evolving understanding of the self that is actualized.

It has been an interest of mine to put myself in a position to define self-actualization in a way that I can find satisfactory. I have not been satisfied with my previous attempts. Thus, I cannot be sure that in a few years I will be satisfied with where I presently stand in this material.

To define the term self-actualization, it is important to tend to the words of the term. Thus, I focus on two aspects of the term: 1) self (What is the self?), and 2) self-actualization (What is self-actualization?).

The Self

What is the Self?

The self is a multi-factorial ontological entity. It arises out of our existence as human beings. It is intra-dependent upon the support of the organism, the environment, and forces in the universe as a whole. It is greatly related internally to various functions of the brain (Damasio, 2003). The self is all I am including my body, my family, my community, my thoughts, experiences, feelings, and emotions. It is not the organism, but the organism is part of the self. It is not the thoughts, consciousness, memories, etc, but these are part of the self. The self is every aspect of one's existence and experience working together to make the self possible.

<u>Self as a Physical Entity</u>

Organism

The self exists because there is an organism. However way we define or view the self, there can be no self without the forces of nature that contribute to the existence of a self.

Whether a person is a creationist or believes the universe fell into existence, assembling on its own, there are forces of physics that contribute to maintaining and sustaining the existence of the universe on a grand scale and which contribute to existence at the molecular level. There are no planets without atoms and other particles. There are forces within and without that make atoms possible and work together and in relationship to every aspect of the organism. Gravity, magnetism, energy, and other forces each contribute to existence and arise because of existence.

The organism does not exist save for being in the universe and there is nothing taking place in the organism that doesn't exist elsewhere in the universe. These forces involve chemistry though chemistry focuses more on the existence of atoms and the like coming together to form elements, molecules, and compounds. Yet, the study of chemistry certainly involves physics. The particles and elements that exist contribute to the inorganic and organic aspects of the universe.

The forces of physics and the elements of chemistry come together to make an organism possible. In this DNA represents this coming together of physics and chemistry. DNA is a complex entity made possible by many forces of physics and chemistry.

In this, there is no life without biology. Biology is the study of the workings of organisms. It explores the relationships of the parts of the organism that make life possible. These parts work together in the case of the human organism all these parts come together to put a unique twist to being a living organism, a self. And thus there is no self without the arrangement of biological components.

A simple picture related to the organism looks like this. Various forces come together to form particles, electrons, protons, nuclei. These come together to form atoms. These atoms can be classed as elements, oxygen, carbon, nitrogen, etc. For a variety of reasons including the need to share or obtain additional electrons, atoms come together and form molecules and/or compounds. Oxygen atoms come together and form O_2. Carbon atoms come together with oxygen atoms to form CO_2. While these two examples are simple, there are an incredible variety of elements, molecules and compounds.

The arrangements become more and more complex and this complexity is captured nicely in DNA which being made up of four basic sugar and phosphate groups, adenine, thymine, guanine, and cytosine, form the basis for life. Sections of these, genes, contribute to the characteristics of the living organism. Yet, DNA is constructed within already existing life forms, cells and the cells' particular parts. While the atoms and basic compounds needed to construct the more complex parts of DNA are plucked from the environment, the more complex parts of DNA are assembled within the cell. A wide variety of elements and molecules are utilized in the formation of cells and its components: nucleus, Golgi bodies, ribosomes, mitochondrion, and cell walls.

For a host of reasons some cells join together in some ways and separate in other ways to form the parts of an organism. For instance my recollection is that the adrenal glands which sit on the kidneys are derived from the same type of cells that produce the brain. During the process of the development of the human organism, these cells that will form the adrenal gland migrate to their appropriate position in the body. In the human organism (an in other similar creatures), cells form the eyes, skin, stomach, heart, spleen, brain, and lungs, etc., etc., etc. All these work together to from a human being.

For the most part, these all in turn contribute something to the ability of the human organism to become a self.

Of course, of significance here is the brain. A myriad of parts, including neurons, synaptic gaps, neurotransmitters, hypothalamus, brain stem, cerebrum, and cerebellum, function in such a way to make the self possible.

Rogers (1951) noted there are those who regard the organism and the self as synonymous. I personally believe there is no self without an organism, though it is possible for there to be an organism without a self.

As I indicated above, I also believe the organism is part of the self, but not the self. I look at "my" hands with "my" eyes. The self is not limited to the organism. The self is the distinctive human experience in relationship to the human organism. These human experiences are in relationship to the organism which includes the brain, the human self, being different from other creatures and organisms, contemplates its existence, considers meaning of life, and uses thought and language (verbal communication) in addition to nonverbal communication. There is plenty of indication that the human being (self) uses his/her intelligence quite differently than other organisms though it is hard to deny that other organisms have intelligence.

Self as an Experiential Entity

Psychology

Having made a connection among self, body, environment, world, and universe, there still remains something different about the self. Other organisms have bodies, environments, worlds, and are part of the universe. Yet, as far was I know they don't think about themselves. They simply do whatever they do as apes, snakes, birds, fish, amoeba, or whatever.

The human being has something different. I am calling that unique aspect of being human a self. For instance, a flea is an organism, but a flea is not and cannot become a human being. I thus reserve the term "self" as a term related to being human.

The self is made possible because of a host of entities. It has an experiential element to it. It in essence transcends the physical world and involves the production of images, memory, thoughts, emotions, and feelings. For instance thoughts, and emotions have no physical existence. Yet, there would be no thoughts or emotions without the physical components that make them possible. We can't touch, see, smell, or hear thoughts and emotions. They transcend the physical domain, but would immediately disappear with the disappearance of the physical domain.

The human being adds its own unique twist to existence and this twist involves the experiences that are part of making the human organism as a self. Rogers (1951) basically stated that the self is "the awareness of being, of functioning" (p. 498). These experiences are related to existence in a variable world of other experiences. "As a result of the interaction with the environment, and particulate as a result of evaluational interaction with others, the structure of self is formed–and organized, fluid, but consistent conceptual pattern of perceptions of characteristics and relationships of the 'I' or the 'me,' together with values attached to these concepts" (p. 498).

Within the realm of experience there arise aspects of the self that are related to personal psychology. One has personal experiences of thinking, memory, intelligence, emotions, and interpretation of feelings—pain, touch, and hunger, etc. (Damasio, 2003). In my thinking, I see psychology as being about thinking, memory, personality, and self, etc.

Related to psychology is one's personal style which I call personality. There are a host of ways to look at personality (Hall & Lindzey, 1993). This personality originates from within the person in response or reaction to the above experiences. A person may tend to behave in certain ways and facilitate certain responses from others. In addition, a person may behave in certain ways in response to similar external behaviors or in spite of external behaviors.

The person in the midst of this has vast resources for creativity for handling various circumstances and situations that may occur. A child can recover from a fall off a bicycle. A person with depression may move toward joy.

Yet, in this, one's resources include external resources. We simply don't exist in a vacuum. We can gain ideas, support, and information from others. Freud and a host of others argued that we are greatly influenced by significant relationships which can even hurt us as we develop. Carl Rogers (1957) acknowledged certain conditions as being "necessary and sufficient" conditions for personal growth. While a person can certainly generate these conditions (acceptance, understanding, and congruence) within him or her self, the ability to do so apparently is enhanced in environments rich with these conditions.

Sociology

There is a rich source of resources external to the self which play roles as Rogers (1951) indicated in helping to form the self. These resources contribute to one's identity. I am a Jew. I am a Russian. I am a black woman. I am smart. I am talented. I push myself past even "my" mind and into the external world and talk about "my" school, "my" job, "my" family, or "my" friends. When something happens to these, something happens to me, to "my" self. I am influenced by these realities. Dorothy Nolte's (1993) poem "Children Learn What They Live" captures this nicely though I will not vouch for the universality of her statements in it. Here are few lines:

"If children live with criticism, they learn to condemn.
If children live with hostility, they learn to fight.
…If children live with tolerance, they learn to be patient.
If children live with encouragement, they learn to be confident…." (p. 85).

The world around the person has a great impact, maybe too much at times, or maybe we are too unaware of the impact at times thinking that our ideas are uniquely ours. These external forces shape us greatly and maybe more so than we shape them. After all we are out numbered. I am only one person in a world of many persons. Thus, a person may tend to be impacted by the world around himself or herself in a certain way depending on the slant of the immediate world surrounding that person.

Yet, it cannot be denied that a person impacts his or her immediate world. A person will tend to present himself or herself in a consistent way to the world around him/her. When my first daughter (Katie) came into the world, and even before she was born, she turned our twosome family upside down. She altered the use of our time, and impacted our activities. She did it in her own unique way.

When my second daughter (Erin) came into that world, she turned the world Katie turned upside down, inside out, altering the threesome's time and activities in yet other ways. She did that in her own unique way.

Their growth and development kept and keeps having an impact on our family's world, upon my "self."

I see no reason not to believe that every human being presents him or her self in his or her own unique style.

Ontology

Here I simply assert that the self is the sum total of one's being. It is one's mental, physical, biological, and experiential being. These come together in existence. Some aspects are readily seen and examined. Other aspects such as thoughts, consciousness can be demonstrated but not actually seen. The body and its parts are only part of being. Kant's assertion, "I think, therefore I am" is also part of being. It is a part of what it means to be human. Thus, the self, the essence of what it means to be human is not limited to thinking, nor to the organism. "The self is comprised of the actual experience of oneself, including thoughts and emotions" (Bower, 1989, p. 6).

Self-Actualization

Self-actualization was defined by Rogers (1989) as the human being's "tendency to grow, to develop, realize its full potential" (p. 137). In (1961), Rogers wrote, "the Individual has within himself the capacity and the tendency, latent if not evident, to move toward maturity" (p. 35). Richard Sharf's (1996) interpretation of Rogers's concept says "self-actualization implies that individuals seek and are capable of healthy development, which leads to full expression of themselves" (p. 217).

Maslow (1968) defined self-actualization "as ongoing actualization of potentials, capacities and talents, as fulfillment of mission (or call, fate, destiny, or vocation), as a fuller knowledge of, and acceptance of, the person's own intrinsic nature, as unceasing trend toward unity, integration or synergy within the person)" (p. 25).

I find that I don't like any of these definitions. They are too oriented toward the idealistic. They fail to capture something of the essence of a person as he or she is in any given moment. Therefore, I propose the following definition. Self-actualization is the process of a self becoming actual and real. In this model, the self-actualization process is an ontological process whereby the self comes into existence. It enables a person to become the person one truly is, rather than an ideal that has not been reached. The person here is always a person that is, although there are always possibilities for change. I also acknowledge in this that the person may not always seek to be the best person he or she can be in any particular moment. I make no assumption that the person is always doing his or her best. However, I am claiming that the person is always him or herself whether or not he or she is doing his/her best.

<u>Characteristics</u>

Bozarth (1998) offerings the following characteristics of self-actualization: the actualization tendency is...

1. Individual and universal
2. Holistic
3. Ubiquitous and constant
4. A directional process
5. Tension increasing
6. The tendency toward autonomy and away from heteronomy
7. Vulnerable to environmental circumstances

These characteristics aren't particularly helpful to defining self-actualization, but they give a sense of the essence of the concept.

I rather like to think of the characteristics of the self-actualization process as including:

1. Resourcefulness
2. Creativity
3. Flexibility
4. Adaptability
5. Interactive
6. Contemplative

None of these is unique to the human experience. However, coupled with the unique capabilities of the human brain to think, reason, and the use language, there is something unique about the actualization process of the human being.

Therapy

Psychotherapy is the providing of a psycho-social atmosphere which contributes to an opportunity for organizing or reorganizing the self (Rogers, 1951, 1986), or for discovering the self one truly is. Rogers (1957) asserted that one of the necessary ingredients for therapy to take place was for the client to be incongruent. If this is true and there is some sort of discrepancy within the client presumably between the self, and the self as perceived, then therapy is about discovering the self that one really is.

Rogers (1951) shared the following observations concerning movement in therapy which I believe captures part of the essence of the organization or reorganization of the self in relationship to therapy. There is change in the:

1. Type of material presented
2. Perception of and attitude toward self
3. Manner of perception
4. Valuing process
5. Therapeutic relationship
6. Personality Structure and Organization

Yet, I don't want to leave therapy just for those who are somehow blocked from the self that truly is and need or want to make a movement in organization or reorganization. Psychotherapy may be about the person who is dissatisfied with the self that one truly is and wishes to change that self. The client may simply not like what he or she sees and experiences and want to change. Therapy, then may be about altering the self so that it becomes more acceptable to the person or to that person's immediate world. The reasons for this may include agreeing with external pressure that change is necessary. For instance, an abusive parent may be pressured to become more compassionate and understanding with his/her children. Another person may be pressured to become more assertive. The person may want to change because he or she feels left out of a significant social life, or is too miserable as the life of the party.

Finally, therapy may not promote long term change at all. A person may be so damaged that significant change may not be evident to anyone. Rogers's (1980) potato-bin illustration didn't show that, in spite of reaching their roots in an effort to survive, the potatoes will eventually rot and fail to produce new potatoes or be useful for human consumption. The person on the back-ward of the hospital may be virtually in a vegetative state and not be able to make any apparent growth other than being able to swallow food if fed. Does this mean that therapy is impossible or insignificant?

I assert and address my answer of "no" with a physical case. When I was involved with my internship in Clinical Pastoral Education, there was an Episcopalian priest who was so severally racked with arthritis that he was bed ridden. He had the worst case of arthritis I had ever seen. His fingers were frozen sideways. A normal hand cannot be put in the position his fingers were in. His joints were so inflamed that movement of any kind was excruciating. Often, he had so much pain that his own bed sheets aggravated the pain.

Every day he was sent for physical therapy in spite of the fact that there was no hope for a cure. I member questioning why a person in that condition was a patient in the rehabilitation center and why was he provided therapy when there was no hope.

What I found out was that, at least during the time of therapy, when they took him down in his own bed because it was too painful to move him to a gurney and then move him again in the physical therapy room, he received some relief from the chronic excruciating pain. That relief was sustained for a brief period. By that, I mean the pain was not as intense as it usually was. However, it was always present.

His other avenue of relief was related to those occasions when the man was able to step into another level of consciousness and not be aware of his pain.

It occurred to me over the years of engaging people who were extremely depressed, anxious, psychotic, or a host of other circumstances that the psychotherapeutic time might be the only part of the day in which some client's receive care, some degree of relief, or some measure of escape from their emotional pain. It might be the only part of the day, where they feel they can experience more fully just how horrible their situation is and this in itself may be a kind of relief in the midst of their atrocity. Perhaps no one else is willing to engage the client in such a way.

The Self in the Real World

Psychotherapy is not the only arena in which people function. It is not even close to being the usual place that people come to know who they are, seek to change who they are, or have to live with who they are. In this, Rogers altered what he called this approach. He called it the Person-Centered Approach. He recognized that the core conditions of empathy, acceptance, and genuineness were valuable in a wide variety of settings in which human growth can occur.

My bias is to do the best job I can in maintaining the core conditions in whatever setting I am in. My bias is so adamant that I have little tolerance for a client-centered perspective which I perceive as limiting the deliberate use of the core conditions to clients in therapy. In this intolerance, I consider myself in a violation of some of the tenants of the approach in that I am intolerant and judgmental. I have simply found that the core conditions can be applied in a host of settings and are indeed successfully presented in other settings allowing for growth and change (Bower, 2001). I have seen churches I have served change as people are allowed to be open about whom they are and the ideas and thoughts they have had in relationship to their faith and church polity. I have seen political panels change when there was an openness to differing positions rather than an attempt to suppress those differences. I have seen nursing unit staffs work out problems in communication and thus change. And this is supported by the observations of others (Bower, 2001).

As is often said, "the bottom line is" getting in touch with the self. That self may be elusive, or may be unsatisfactory, or so wounded that it cannot be healed. The person-centered approach is about opening the door the self that one truly is.

REFERENCES

Bower, D. W. (1985). Assumptions and attitudes of the Rogerian person-centered approach to counseling: Implications for pastoral counseling. Unpublished manuscript, Columbia Theological Seminary, Decatur, GA.

Bower, D. W. (1986). The attributes of five person-centered therapists. Unpublished doctoral dissertation, University of Georgia, Athens, GA.

Bower, D. W. (2001). *The person-centered approach: Applications for living.* New York: iUniverse.

Bozarth, J. (1998). *Person-centered therapy: A revolutionary paradigm.* Ross-on-Wye: PCCS Books.

Brodley, B. T. (1999). The actualizing tendency concept in client-centered theory. *The Person-Centered Journal,* 6(2), 108-120.

Damasio, A. (2003). *The feelings of what happens: body and emotion in the making of consciousness.* San Diego: A Harvest Book—Hardcourt, Inc.

Hall, C. S., & Lindzey, G. (1978). *Theories of personality.* New York: John Wiley & Sons.

Nolte, D.L. (1993). Children learn what they live. In J. Canfield, & M. V. Hansen (Eds.). *Chicken Soup for the Soul: 101 Stories to Open the Heart and Rekindle the Spirit.* Deerfield Beach, Florida: Health Communications.

Rogers, C. R. (1951). *Client-centered therapy.* Boston: Houghton Mifflin.

Rogers, C. R. (1961). *On becoming a person.* Boston: Houghton Mifflin.

Rogers, C. R. (1980). *A way of being.* Boston: Houghton Mifflin.

Rogers, C. R. (1986). Rogers, Kohut, and Erickson: A personal perspective on some similarities and differences. *Person-Centered Review,* 1(2), 125-140.

Rogers, C. R. (1989). The client-centered/person-centered approach to therapy. In H. Kirschenbaum, & V. L. Henderson (Eds.), *The Carl Rogers Reader* (pp. 135-152). Boston: Houghton Mifflin. (Reprinted from psychotherapist's case book, pp. 197-208, by I. Kutash, & A. Wolf (Eds.), 1986, New York: Jossey-Bass).

Is That All There Is to Counseling and Psychotherapy?

C. H. Patterson

Psychology is currently experiencing a renewed interest in cognition. This interest is evidenced in almost every field of psychology from child and developmental psychology, through neuropsychology to behaviorism and counseling or psychotherapy. As is often the case, such movements tend to gather a momentum which leads to a swinging of the pendulum to an extreme position, often in part as a reaction to, and from, an extreme swing in the opposite direction. We have been going through a period in psychotherapy, indeed in the entire human relations area, in which there have been many practitioners focusing on emotional expression almost to an exclusion of cognition or thinking. While a corrective trend is no doubt desirable, it would appear to be undesirable to go to an extreme.

The purpose of this paper is to serve as a corrective to what I perceive as a movement which is in the process of becoming extreme. The movement appears to be leading to a position which is characterized by one or more of the following propositions: (1) the apparent complexities of counseling or psychotherapy can be reduced to the more simple and better understood, and more easily acquired and practiced, methods of teaching and instruction; (2) counseling or psychotherapy is the same as education or teaching; (3) education or teaching is thus a substitute for counseling or psychotherapy.

Before raising some questions about these assumptions (or conclusions), let me establish my credentials as one who has not rejected the importance of teaching or education in personal growth and development or as a remedial process (re-education) and one who has not drawn a sharp line between or education and counseling or psychotherapy.

In 1939 I wrote a paper entitled "Therapy as Re-education." It was never published, although I recall submitting it to at least one journal (I have been unable to find any record in my files although I do have a copy of the paper). In 1969, in my Preface to one of Carkhuff's books (Patterson, 1969), I welcomed evidence that direct training in the conditions of good interpersonal relations was more effective than psychotherapy. I continued: "Perhaps therapy is not necessary! What we may need is direct training or education of everyone in the conditions of good human relations—not only 'normal' people and children, but the emotionally disturbed as well." In 1971 (Patterson, 1971) I commented favorably on developments toward the teaching of human relations, suggesting that such teaching should begin in elementary schools. This suggestion was developed in my book on humanistic education (Patterson, 1973a), a concept and movement which incorporates psychological education.

That there is some relationship between education and teaching and counseling or psychotherapy is not a new idea. As I recall, my 1939 paper was rejected for publication because its thesis was not new. In my 1939 paper I wrote: "all therapy can be described and understood or interpreted in terms of the principles of learning." There has been a large and continuing literature on psychotherapy as a learning process, dating back to at least 1946 (See Patterson, 1973b, p. 86, for references). Ellis' rational-emotive psychotherapy, dating back to 1955, is almost entirely a cognitive, teaching or tutoring process. Much of behavior therapy is also essentially direct teaching. Even psychiatry is being influenced by the cognitive trend (e.g., Beck, 1976). To say that psychotherapy involves learning, however, does not mean that it also involves teaching, since teaching is not necessary for learning.

The problem is one of conceptualizing in an integrated rather than either/or manner the relationship between cognitive and affective approaches to the influencing or changing of human behavior (and here I include feelings—attitudes and beliefs—as behavior). Certainly it should be axiomatic that cognition and affect cannot be separated, except for heuristic purposes, since all behavior includes elements of each in varying proportions. The ubiquitous either/or fallacy constitutes perhaps the greatest obstacle to progress, in thinking and in practice, e.g., the treatment or prevention argument.

Is Teaching Simpler, Easier and More Efficient than Counseling or Psychotherapy? Part of the attraction of the movement toward redefining the role of the counselor as that of a teacher appears to be the belief that teaching is easier than counseling. Counselors are confused by the many theories and approaches in counseling or psychotherapy, and see teaching as something that is clear, simple, and easily mastered. But this is certainly not the case, as even a slight acquaintance with the literature on teaching and instruction shows. It is paradoxical that, although education and teaching date back centuries beyond counseling or psychotherapy, there is currently nothing that would warrant the designation of a theory of instruction (Patterson, 1977b). Although psychotherapy in its early forms was much more primitive than early education, being dominated by superstition and the supernatural, it has progressed to the point where, although there are numerous theories, it is possible to identify some common basic elements (Patterson, 1973b, 1974b).

One of the reasons for the retarded development of teaching and instruction has been the focus upon cognition and the failure to recognize that learning is not simply a cognitive process. In this area, rather than learning theory contributing to counseling theory, it is the latter which can contribute to learning theory and instruction. There is evidence that progress is being made in this direction, as shown by the development of humanistic education. There are other difficulties with humanistic education as it is popularly being developed, however, one of which is the attempt to package affective education in cognitive curriculum containers (Patterson, 1973b, 1977a). But as the affective aspects of teaching are recognized, it is becoming apparent that the conditions of cognitive learning are the same as the conditions of learning or change in counseling or psychotherapy. Paradoxically, as education moves toward counseling or psychotherapy, the current trend of defining counseling as teaching moves toward traditional education.

As far as the teaching of mental hygiene, psychological adjustment, or human relations is concerned, the record is extremely poor. Efforts going back for forty years have had little if any success. One of the main reasons is the method of teaching. Arbuckle (1976) notes that "the history of trying to "teach" a person to be a more effective human being is about as dismal as the history of traditional psychoanalysis in trying to "cure" a person of a "sickness""

He takes a dim view of current efforts to teach human relations skills: "I have known many effective people who possess many of the 'skills' of being an effective person. The trouble is that they are ineffective people who have been taught mechanistic skills of being effective." I have visions of a world in which people go around "practicing" their so-called "skills" on each other. Nothing could be more phony or inhuman.

However, it is possible to teach people to relate to each other in a more human way. The focus must be on philosophy and attitudes, not upon skills. The point is that traditional methods of cognitive instruction will not be effective. Effective teaching is not simpler or easier than counseling or psychotherapy. In fact it requires some of the same attitudes or conditions.

Is Counseling or Psychotherapy, then, the Same as Teaching? As in attempts to distinguish between counseling and psychotherapy (Patterson, 1974a, 1974b), confusion reigns in the writing of those who attempt to equate counseling with teaching. Early writers were wont to say that the only or major difference between teaching and counseling is in the subject matter; that is, in counseling the subject matter is the student himself. This results in the paradox that in counseling, the student rather than the teacher is the expert on the subject matter. I have often suggested, facetiously, that the greatest similarity between teaching and counseling or psychotherapy is that they both have a fifty minute hour.

The ridiculous level to which we have come is illustrated by the statement that "the function of therapeutic and developmental counseling is being taken on by the classroom teacher. Counselors will shift their priorities to teaching and training parents, students, school staff, and lay people to use counseling skills" (Pine, 1974). It is not clear whether this involves equating teaching with counseling or psychotherapy, but it consists of a role reversal. We should then call teachers counselors and counselors teachers. A parenthetical comment on so-called developmental counseling might be noted here. Developmental counseling appears to be a form of teaching. But its practitioners apparently need know little if anything about the complex and confusing literature and research in developmental psychology. It is sufficient that they be familiar with the stages of Erikson and Kohlberg, with a light smattering of Piaget.

Much of the difficulty has arisen from the efforts to make counseling something other than psychotherapy. The result has been that definitions of counseling have made the counselor a teacher. It may very well be that what most counselors do (particularly in schools) is teaching rather than counseling. But the fact that many counselors are actually engaged in individual teaching or tutoring activities does not mean that counseling is teaching. Nor is it necessarily true that they are effective teachers. If counseling is identical with teaching, then it would seem to be unnecessary and undesirable to have two words for the same thing. But counselors in schools prefer, for a number of reasons (including status and salary), not to be classified as teachers. Thus there are attempts to differentiate counseling from teaching, with the result that counseling then becomes indistinguishable from psychotherapy. The development of the concept of psychological education, which essentially defines the subject matter which counselors would teach, seems to be an attempt to resolve this dilemma. At any rate, the writing in this area is messy, with writers using language as Humpty Dumpty did in Lewis Carroll's "Through the Looking Glass:" "When I use a word it means just what I choose it to mean."

But there are differences between teaching and counseling. Teaching usually involves classroom size groups; counseling is on a one-to-one or small group basis. Teaching involves standard subject matter; the content of counseling is unstandardized, and is personal and unique to the individual. Teaching is usually relatively highly structured, following a lesson plan; counseling is usually relatively unstructured, following the client's programming. Teaching is more impersonal, while counseling is more personal. Teaching focuses upon cognitive aspects or elements; counseling emphasizes or focuses upon affective aspects. In teaching, as has been increasingly recognized (and demonstrated) the relationship between the teacher and student is important as the medium of teaching; in counseling the relationship is the essence (often sufficient). In teaching the emphasis or focus is upon cognitive development; in counseling the emphasis or focus is upon affective development.

Is Teaching a Substitute for or Interchangeable with Counseling? If, as clearly seems to be the case, counseling and teaching are not the same, then it would appear that they are not interchangeable. Therefore, the emphasis upon choosing between one or the other is an example of the either/or fallacy. There is a place for both, and a need for both. To insist that counselors abandon counseling and engage only in teaching is to limit or restrict the availability of counseling for those who need it. Of course it is desirable that those who call themselves counselors but actually engage in teaching make it clear to their clientele that they do not engage in counseling.

The relevant question becomes that of when is teaching appropriate, and when is counseling the preferred mode. This question has not been addressed. Education or teaching has been proclaimed as "the preferred mode," without adequate consideration of the question "for what?"

The Limits of Education as a Preferred Mode of Treatment. Many of those who advocate teaching as a preferred mode of treatment appear to see it as a panacea, which has no limits and which makes counseling or psychotherapy obsolete. Authier et al. (1975) note the "widespread advocacy and logical appeal of an educational approach to the treatment of psychological disturbance." Yet they list the major elements of a traditional direct teaching model as "providing instruction and information, providing models, providing evaluation and feedback on performance and coordinating the overall program," with no mention of the affective and relationship elements. Others, of course recognize these elements—Carkhuff's model particularly emphasizes the necessity of the core conditions (empathic understanding, respect and therapeutic genuineness (Carkhuff, 1971; Carkhuff & Berenson, 1976).

The optimism about education replacing counseling or psychotherapy appears to rest upon several studies involving the teaching of human relations skills to psychiatric patients (Goldstein, 1973; Pierce & Drasgow, 1969; Vitalo, 1971). These studies involving a very small number of patients bear an enormous burden. The patients in the Pierce and Drasgow study were chronic patients who, it was believed, "could not meaningfully participate in, or benefit from, programs of individual or group psychotherapy." (But see Rogers, Gendlin, Kiesler &

Truax, 1967, for evidence that such patients as well as highly disturbed patients can be reached by psychotherapy.) In the most extensive study, that of Goldstein, half of the 18 studies conducted yielded negative results.

The fact that selected psychiatric patients can be taught interpersonal skills does not mean that all patients are accessible to such teaching, or that such teaching is all that is necessary for change or improvement in the patient's condition.

1. Education as a planned, structured, cognitively oriented intervention is not appropriate, or possible with clients who are emotionally disturbed or upset by current situations, problems or experiences. They are in no mood to attend to and benefit from didactic instruction, even from manifesting high levels of the core conditions. Learning is most likely to take place when the learner is ready and sees the content as relevant.

2. Most clients who come to counselors or therapists have specific problems which need to be expressed and explored. Though these problems usually involve interpersonal relationships, they are highly specific and involve personal content with which the client is preoccupied and which he must explore.

3. The process of exploration and learning is a uniquely personal one, which is best facilitated in an understanding, spontaneous relationship rather than a planned, structured, process directed by the instructor and covering predetermined subject matter. Teaching usually takes place in groups, and a planned program of instruction is not likely to be relevant and meaningful to all clients at the same time, or necessarily for any one of them at the time it occurs in the lesson plan, even when the subject matter is personal or human relations.

4. While most clients manifest problems in interpersonal relations, these are usually the result of the way they have been or are treated by others. While changes in the way others react to the client occur as the client changes his ways of relating to them, it would appear to be more direct and efficient to teach significant others the principles of good interpersonal relationships. (This of course is recognized by Carkhuff [1971] and much is being done in this area.)

5. Teaching inevitably places the instructor in a position of an expert and an authority, an initiator and programmer of the process. And inevitably this deprives the client, at least to some extent, of being the initiator and programmer, and of being responsible for the content and process of learning. Thus, one of the desirable outcomes of counseling or psychotherapy, the development of responsibility and independence, or a responsible independence (Patterson, 1959) is hindered or inhibited.

6. For most clients who come to a counselor or psychotherapist the relationship is sufficient for positive personality and behavior change. They do not need information, instruction, or skill training, or if they do they can obtain it for themselves elsewhere. What they need from the counselor or therapist is a non-

threatening relationship in which they can come to their own decisions and resolve their own problems. They learn decision making by making decisions, and problem solving by solving their own problems. They learn to take responsibility for themselves by being required to take responsibility in the relationship. Too many counselors have too little confidence in their clients to allow them to learn to be responsible. And they have too little confidence in themselves to realize or learn the power of a facilitative relationship. Most failures in counseling or psychotherapy derive from the inability of the therapist to provide a facilitative relationship. The insecure therapist who cannot provide such a relationship resorts to teaching. Although he may succeed in teaching something to some extent, he fails to help the client to learn to help himself.

The most significant learning occurs without direct instruction or teaching, This is true outside of therapy as well as in therapy. The best education, paradoxically, does not involve didactic instruction or teaching. Theory and research in counseling or psychotherapy has led to a change in the concept of the teacher as an instructor to the concept of the teacher as a facilitator of learning. Part of the basic, common drive toward growth and development (toward self-actualization) is the drive or motivation to learn. Thus learning naturally and normally occurs in an environment which provides the conditions for learning. These conditions are the same as those which lead to positive behavior change (learning) in counseling or psychotherapy.

Rogers writes that "It seems to me that anything that can be taught to another is relatively inconsequential and has little or no significant influence on behavior.... I have come to feel that the only learning which significantly influences behavior is self-discovered, self-appropriated learning" (Rogers, 1969, p. 153, italics in original). "The initiation of such learning", he writes, "rests not upon the teaching skills of the leader, not upon his curriculum planning, not upon his use of audio-visual aids, not upon the programmed learning he utilizes, not upon his lectures and presentations, not upon an abundance of books, though each of these might at one time or another be utilized as an important resource. No, the facilitation of significant learning rests upon certain attitudinal qualities which exist in the personal relationship between the facilitator and the learner." (Rogers, 1969, pp. 105-106).

Thus, it is the relationship which is basic in the teaching-learning process. The counselor cannot escape from the responsibility of providing a facilitative relationship by becoming a teacher. The poor counselor will be a poor teacher.

The crucial element in cognitive learning is the affective relationship, as it is in affective learning. A purely cognitive approach to learning is not sufficient (Patterson, 1968). Didactic instruction is not enough, and not necessary. Education must be redefined; rather than being equated with direct teaching and instruction, it must be equated with a relationship which facilitates learning. When this is done, education may then be broad enough to include counseling or psychotherapy (though there will be differences related to the differences in the condition of the learner) because it has incorporated into itself what we have learned about learning from counseling or psychotherapy.

What, then, is the place of direct teaching or instruction? As a purely cognitive, didactic process, there is very little place. Dissemination of information is more efficiently done by other methods. The recognition of how little is learned in the traditional classroom should demonstrate the ineffectiveness of teaching, and should be sufficient to lead us to resist reducing counseling to teaching.

But education, as the facilitation of significant learning, is another matter. Humanistic education, which insists on the inclusion of affective development as well as cognitive development in education, is very important. It insists that every child should be educated in the area of interpersonal relations. Since many if not most of the problems which clients bring to counselors or therapists involve difficulties in interpersonal relations, education can be preventive of if not most of these problems.

But there are, and will be for a long time, those who already have problems, who are not ready to use a standard or traditional teaching approach, but who do respond to a pure relationship approach, which is both necessary and sufficient. Counseling or psychotherapy is necessary where teaching or education, including parenting, has been inadequate or has failed, leaving the individual in a disturbed, confused state where traditional teaching is no longer appropriate or even possible.

Summary. This paper has presented an analysis of the current trend toward education as the preferred mode of treatment for all emotionally disturbed clients including psychiatric patients. Confusions regarding terminology were explored, While those who advocate viewing counseling or psychotherapy as education appear to believe that teaching is less complex and easier than counseling or psychotherapy, in actuality we know less about effective teaching than we do about effective counseling or psychotherapy. It is paradoxical that while these advocates are attracted to education or teaching because of its cognitive elements, education is entering a period in which the affective elements in teaching and learning, both in method and as subject matter, are being recognized. Research on the components of facilitative interpersonal relationships has been extended from counseling or psychotherapy to teaching, and indicates that the same conditions which are necessary for change in psychotherapy are important in significant cognitive learning.

Thus the attempt to substitute traditional teaching for counseling or psychotherapy may be considered a regressive movement. Rather, we may say that the future lies in substituting counseling or psychotherapy—or its essential elements—for traditional teaching. Such education, involving not only cognitive but affective development including interpersonal relations, may well, in some distant future, make the practice of counseling or psychotherapy almost unnecessary. But in the meantime, both better education and counseling or psychotherapy, both prevention and remediation, are necessary. And while there are common elements in effective teaching and effective counseling or psychotherapy, there are significant differences related to the nature and condition of the learner.

C.H. Patterson's works have enriched the science and art of counseling. He has served as mentor and exemplar for generations of students, his standards of excellence have inspired many, and his dedication to the best of counseling psychology has placed him among the leaders of psychotherapy for decades. He has earned the highest respect from his peers, who presented him with The Leona Tyler Award in 1994 for outstanding contributions to education, training, supervision, and practice in counseling psychology. Doctor Patterson lives in Asheville, North Carolina.

REFERENCES

Arbuckle, D. S. (1976). Comment. *Personnel and Guidance Journal,* 54, 434.

Authier, J., Gustafson, K., Guerrney, B. Jr., Kasdorf, J. A. (1975). The psychological practitioner as a teacher: A Theoretical-historical review. *The Counseling Psychologist,* 5 (2), 31-50.

Beck, A. T. (1976). *Cognitive therapy and the emotional disorders.* New York: International Universities Press.

Carkhuff, R. R. (1971). Training as a preferred mode of treatment. *Journal of Counseling Psychology,* 18, 123-131.

Carkhuff, R. R., & Berenson, B. G. (1976). *Teaching as treatment: An introduction to counseling and psychotherapy.* Amherst, Mass.: Human Resources Development Press.

Goldstein, A. (1973). *Structured learning therapy: Toward a psychotherapy for the poor.* New York: Academic Press.

Patterson, C. H. (1939). Therapy as reeducation. Unpublished paper.

Patterson, C. H. (1959). *Counseling and psychotherapy: Theory and practice.* New York: Harper and Row.

Patterson, C. H. (1968). Is cognition sufficient? In Parker, C. (Ed.) *Counseling theories and counselor education.* Boston: Houghton Mifflin.

Patterson, C. H. (1969). Preface. In Carkhuff, R. *Helping and human relations. Vol. II. Practice and research.* New York: Holt, Rinehart & Winston.

Patterson, C. H. (1971). Education and training as the preferred mode of treatment. *The Counseling Psychologist,* 3 (1), 77-79.

Patterson, C. H. (1973a). *Humanistic education.* Englewood Cliffs, N.J.: Prentice-Hall.

Patterson, C. H. (1973b). *Theories of counseling and psychotherapy.* 2nd ed. New York: Harper & Row.

Patterson, C. H. (1974a). Distinctions and commonalities between counseling and psychotherapy. In Farwell, G. F., Gamsky, N. R., & Mathieu-Couglan, P. *The counselor's handbook:* New York: Intext, pp. 13-26.

Patterson, C. H. (1974b). *Relationship counseling and psychotherapy.* New York: Harper & Row.

Patterson, C. H. (1977a). Insights about persons: Psychological foundations of humanistic and affective education. In L. M. Berman and J. A. Roderick (Eds.), *Feeling, valuing, and the art of growing: Insights into the affective.* Washington, D.C.: Association for Supervision and Curriculum Development.

Patterson, C. H. (1977b). *Foundations for a theory of instruction and educational psychology*. New York: Harper & Row.

Pierce, R. & Drasgow, J. (1969). Teaching facilitative interpersonal functioning to psychiatric patients. *Journal of Counseling Psychology*, 16, 295-298.

Pine, G. J. (1974). Let's give away school counseling. *School Counselor*, 22, 94-99.

Rogers, C. R. (1969). *Freedom to learn*. Columbus, Ohio: Merrill.

Vitalo, R. (1970). The effect of interpersonal functioning in a conditioning paradigm. *Journal of Counseling Psychology*, 17, 141-144.

On Becoming a Nondirective Psychotherapist

Louis B. Fierman, M.D.

Most "schools" of psychotherapy and psychoanalysis rely on directive, interpretive and pedagogic activity as the principal effort of the therapist. These directive and "insight" oriented therapies have as their common denominator a structured authoritarian relationship between patient or client and therapist. It is tacitly agreed that, in a sense, the patient suffers directly or indirectly from a lack of knowledge about himself; or, to be more precise, about that part of himself which is suppressed, repressed, preconscious or unconscious. Furthermore, that the therapist is more familiar with that part of the patient than the patient is himself; and that, finally, if the therapist can successfully impart his esoteric knowledge of the patient to the patient and perhaps assist him or her by imparting additional relevant knowledge, the patient will use the new-found information to cope with and integrate these heretofore hidden aspects of himself so as to become healthier and happier. In addition to promoting "insight," the therapist can also help the patient by offering directly or indirectly strategic and appropriate direction, guidance, advice and suggestions.

However, some psychotherapists, trained and working within such a structured, strategic, insight or directive framework of psychotherapy, become dissatisfied and disillusioned with these premises. After exhausting the many rationalizations available to account for treatment failures, the conscientious psychotherapist arrives at a turning point in which these basic issues are themselves at stake. Many prominent therapists have gradually shifted and promoted therapies that deviate partially or completely from the Freudian analytic, insight-oriented or directive approach. As an alternative they frequently focus on the here-and-now relationship between therapist and patient rather than on the history and pathogenesis of the patient's mental disorder, and in some cases have abandoned directive activity entirely in performing psychotherapy.

Hellmuth Kaiser, Peter Lomas and Carl Rogers were three such therapists. They all began their careers as psychotherapists using structured, technique-oriented, directive approaches in therapy; but became disenchanted with directive psychotherapy and developed similar models of nondirective psychotherapy that have influenced the practice of psychotherapy throughout the world. As Peter Lomas put it succinctly, they all underwent "departure from Freud." (Lomas, 1981, p. 3)

Hellmuth Kaiser graduated from the Berlin Psychoanalytic Institute in 1929 and was trained to be an orthodox Freudian psychoanalyst. However, he was much influenced by Wilhelm Reich, one of his teachers. Reich taught that psychoanalytic therapy was frequently ineffective because the patient's resistance to change was ingrained in his or her character and personality. He advocated that formal analysis should first be preceded by so-called "character analysis,"in which the analyst would confront the patient face-to-face with observations of the patient's overt and covert attitudinal resistances (Reich, 1949).

Kaiser, however, found that therapy became even more effective if, instead of reverting back to orthodox analysis as Reich had taught, he would continue throughout the therapy to confront the patient face-to-face with his overt attitudinal and incongruous communicative behavior. After years of experience, Kaiser gradually became convinced that confrontations seemed to reinforce patients' dependant behavior. He then decided to abandon confrontations, and instead, to simply offer to his patients a here-and-now, non-confrontational, nonjudgmental, nondirective, interactive, communicative-intimacy relationship. He described his gradual evolution to a completely nondirective therapy in his monograph: The Universal Symptom of the Psychoneuroses: a Search for the Conditions of Effective Psychotherapy (Kaiser, 1965a)..

The Kaiserian therapist disavows as therapeutic activity any explicit pedagogy, interpretation, confrontation or strategic maneuvers. The patient is regarded as being literally free to do in the therapy session whatever he or she pleases. The only limitations are those determined by the therapist's personal needs and interests, such as time, financial arrangements or self-protection. Beyond the therapist's personal limitations, the situation and the relationship are left essentially free and unstructured, and the therapist's activity becomes simply sharing with the patient those of his reactions to the patient's behavior that he deems appropriate.

Kaiser regarded dependency as the core psychopathology of psychoneuroses and he designed his therapy to be nondirective to avoid reinforcing the basic dependency of the patient. "Cure" of the patient was to be achieved by the therapist offering the patient a relationship which I have come to call "communicative-intimacy" (Fierman, 1997). The basic assumption of Kaiserian therapy is that consistent nondirective "genuine" behavior and communication on the part of the therapist is all that is "necessary and sufficient" to effect a cure. This concept is analogous to Carl Rogers' concept of "congruence" as an essential condition for psychotherapists. In this therapy the only "rules" are that the patient be physically present with an intact central nervous system, and that the therapist not withdraw psychologically from his or her patient. The Kaiserian model of therapy seems to meet all the criteria for being identical with Carl Rogers' client-centered therapy.

Similar to both Kaiser and Rogers, Peter Lomas, a prominent psychoanalyst in Cambridge, England, also abandoned orthodox psychoanalysis and advocated instead a "personal psychotherapy." In his book, The Case for a Personal Psychotherapy (Lomas, 1981), his rhetoric is analogous to the principles of Rogers' client-centered therapy and Kaiser's communicative-intimacy therapy.

In his book Lomas described what he thought a therapist should not do: "The therapist should not, in a polite or conventional way, smooth over difficulties or (worse) humor the patient or adopt a patronizing bedside manner; nor should he be committed to an opposite dogma—a relentless pursuit of the truth at all costs on all occasions, with an accompanying need to open up old wounds in the interests of theoretical rigor; his primary aim should not be to understand the patient, nor to learn from him, nor to enlarge the frontiers of science through his studies of him, nor to assuage his own loneliness or to seek a substitute for child, spouse, parent or lover. He should not use the patient to treat, vicariously, his own neurosis or as a captive audience for his own particular brand of theory....The perspective I am here proposing for psychotherapy is...embarrassingly unspecific....it refers to a situation in which one person is aiming to help another to grow by offering him a relationship that has much in common with those in ordinary living but takes place in an unusual context" (Lomas, 1981, p. 43-44).

Lomas also urged spontaneity and genuineness as crucial qualities for psychotherapists' responses to their patients: "...I have used the term 'spontaneity' to indicate a quality of response that comes—insofar as this is possible—from the core of one's being rather than behavior that has been rehearsed according to a plan, strategy, or theory. It seems likely that, being unrestrained, the spontaneous mode of being would be less of an effort. The difference is akin to that between a formal dinner party in which one feels the need to behave in an acceptable way and meeting an old friend with whom one can leave one's pretenses behind. Such a meeting is not a scientific search for truth but, in some ways, there is more likely to be truth around" (Lomas, 1999, p. 91).

In his book, <u>The Limitations of Interpretation /What's Wrong With Psychoanalysis</u>, (Lomas, 1987, p. 4), Lomas disavowed analytic interpretation: "Explanation and interpretation are means by which we may attempt to control and diminish the full force of being." In addition he advocated "intimacy" rather than "insight" as a goal of therapy: "....the most apparent impairment (in patients) is an inability to make sufficiently close and realistic relationships with others. It is primarily for this reason that people consult psychotherapists....a major task of the therapist is to help his patients towards a greater capacity for intimacy."(Ibid, p. 69).

Finally we come to the great Carl Rogers, the third of the trio of therapists under discussion, all of whom independently arrived at similar innovative, nondirective, humanistic, nonauthoritarian therapies.

Carl Rogers was raised in a fundamentalist evangelical farm family, the fourth of six children. In his autobiography, <u>On Becoming a Person</u>, he tersely characterizes his early years: "—a very strict and uncompromising religious and ethical atmosphere—parents were very controlling of our behavior." (Rogers, 1961). He considered theology as a career but then trained as a Freudian psychoanalytically-oriented child psychologist at Columbia University. In 1928 he joined the staff of the Rochester Child Study Department and was influenced by the teachings of Otto Rank to abandon orthodox psychoanalysis. He progressively moved away from any approach in therapy that was coercive and developed and published his initial concepts of "client centered therapy" in his book <u>Counseling and Psychotherapy</u> (Rogers, 1942). He was then much influenced by the concept of the "actualizing tendency" promoted by Maslow and others (Maslow 1956), and nondirectiveness became the *sine qua non* of Rogerian psychotherapy. He replaced the directiveness of Freud, Otto Rank and other insight-oriented psychoanalytic psychotherapists with what he called "nondirective acceptance." However, he actually was not completely nondirective at that time. Instead, he advocated that the therapist refrain from interactive activity and instead strive to encourage continued catharsis in order to promote the patient's self actualization.

In his book <u>Client Centered Therapy</u> (1951) he stated: "The therapist endeavors to keep himself out as a separate person…the counselor being depersonalized for the purposes of therapy into being the client's other self." But over the years Rogers gradually abandoned self-restraint and finally advocated his three "core conditions" for effective therapy: 1) The therapist's unconditional positive regard for the client, 2) The therapist's empathic understanding of the client, and 3) The therapist's congruence. In the 60's he finally advocated as therapy offering the patient a full, open, spontaneous, sharing, empathic and congruent relationship. Rogers wrote: "I had come to recognize quite fully that the therapist must be present as a person in the relationship if therapy is to take place" (Evans, 1975, p.25). Later he added:"I find that when I am closest to my inner intuitive self...whatever I do seems to be full of healing...simply my *presence* is releasing and helpful to the other." (Rogers, 1980, p. 129)

Conclusion:

This paper has discussed three prominent therapists who underwent a shift from directive to nondirective therapy; Hellmuth Kaiser, Peter Lomas and Carl Rogers. However, a review of their careers does not reveal exactly just how, why or when that shift occurred. Why, in contrast to most of their professional colleagues and contemporaries, did they become dissatisfied with their previous directive orientation, and why did they end up with such similar humanistic, egalitarian and nondirective therapies? To answer that question we can only speculate as to how their life experiences influenced them to change.

Hellmuth Kaiser was born into and grew up in a well-to-do upper middle class intellectual professional German family. He served in the German army during WWI, and on his return he trained and became a Freudian psychoanalyst. But the anti-Semitic ravages of Hitler's brutal Naziism drove him out of Germany, a stateless, penniless refugee who made his way to Israel and then to the USA, sponsored by Karl Menninger. Perhaps his anger toward his ungrateful, bigoted and authoritarian fatherland helped to fuel his rebellion from authoritarian Freudian psychoanalysis.

Peter Lomas received his M.D. at Manchester University in England, and was a general practitioner before entering the London Institute of Psychoanalysis. He gradually became disillusioned with orthodox analysis after studying the works of Buber and other existential philosophers and therapists, and cites these authors and teachers as persuading him to "depart from Freud."

Carl Rogers experienced in his childhood excessive parental control and religious constrictions, and this may well have contributed to his later aversion to coercion and his discarding all strategic, goal-directed activity from his therapies. Another possible and plausible answer to the riddle of accounting for this shift of these and other therapists to a nondirective, humanistic therapy came from my wife, Ella Yensen Fierman, a clinical psychologist and psychotherapist: "I think they were influenced by their patients," she speculated, "particularly those patients who were able to express their desire to have an egalitarian, open, genuine, nondirective, communicative-intimacy relationship with their therapists. Therapy is a two-way street. Patients can and do influence their therapists and sometimes even free them from their authoritarian constraints."

Her insightful statement reminded me of Hellmuth Kaiser's short play "Emergency" (Kaiser, 1962). Kaiser wrote this playlet to illustrate his contention that the active ingredient of effective psychotherapy was the communicative relationship between therapist and patient and not a function of their relative status or expertise. In the play an imposter patient treats a therapist psychotherapeutically as part of a strategy secretly arranged by the therapist's wife. But I believe the same scenario could just as well have occurred even if the patient were an actual patient who decided to treat his therapist without being hired to do so by a third party.

Irvin Yalom (2002) also has written about occasions when patients have treated their therapists psychotherapeutically. Similarly, Peter Lomas wrote: "The dependence of patients is often the most hazardous ordeal which a psychotherapist has to face." (1981. p. 145). He cites instances when he felt pressured by his patients to become more open, personal and communicative.

Martin Buber maintained that in an I-Thou relationship there is "healing in the meeting" that promotes improved mental health in both patient and therapist and makes the experience of psychotherapy gratifying and nurturing (Buber, 1970).

Louis B. Fierman, M. D. is a former president of the Connecticut Psychiatric Society, and a former Chief of the Psychiatric Service at the West Haven Veterans Administration Medical Center, and a former Medical Director of Elmcrest Psychiatric Institute.

REFERENCES

Buber, M.(1970). *I and Thou.* trans. W. Kaufman {from Buber, M. (1923). *Ich und Du.* Leipzig: Insel-Verlag.}. New York: Charles Scribner and Sons.

Evans, R. I. (1975). *Carl Rogers; The Man and His Ideas.* New York: E. P. Dulton Paperback.

Fierman, L. B. (1997). *The Therapist Is the Therapy.* Northvale, New Jersey: Jason Aronson.

Kaiser, H. (1962). Emergency. *Psychiatry,* 25, 97-118.

Kaiser, H (1965a). The universal symptom of the psychoneuroses: A search for the conditions of effective psychotherapy. In *Effective Psychotherapy / The Contribution of Hellmuth Kaiser,* L. B. Fierman (Ed.). New York: Free Press/Macmillan, pp. 14-171.

Lomas, P. (1981). *The Case for a Personal Psychotherapy.* Oxford: Oxford University Press.

Lomas, P. (1987). *The Limits of Interpretation / What's Wrong With Psychoanalysis.* New York: Penquin Books.

Lomas, P. (1999). *Doing Good? Psychotherapy Out Of Its Depth.* Oxford: Oxford University Press

Maslow, A. H. (1956). Self-actualizing People: A Study of Psychological Health. In *The Self: Explorations in Personal Growth.* C. E. Moustakas (Ed.). New York: Harper & Row.

Reich, W. (1949). *Character Analysis.* New York: Orgone Institute Press.

Rogers, C. R (1942). *Counseling and Psychotherapy.* Boston: Houghton Miflin

Rogers, C. R. (1951). *Client-Centered Therapy, Its Current Practice, Implications and Theory.* Boston: Houghton Mifflin.

Rogers, C. R.(1961). *On Becoming A Person.* Boston: Houghton Mifflin.

Rogers, C. R. (1980). *A Way of Being.* Boston: Houghton Mifflin.

Yalom, I. D. (2002). On Being Helped By Your Patient. In *The Gift of Therapy.* New York: Harper Collins Publishers.

Search for the Locus of the Universal Symptom: Re-examination of Hellmuth Kaiser's *Duplicity*

Jerry Krakowski

Wilhelm Reich, a member of Freud's inner circle, proposed that a first step in the course of treating neurotic patients is to pay more attention to their behavior, and subsequently proceed with their analysis.[1] By suspending concerns with the patient's pathology in the initial phase of treatment, he deviated from traditional psychoanalysis. Hellmuth Kaiser, his student, went beyond Reich by proposing that paying attention to the patient's behavior, in its totality, is the only step in treating patients—there is no other analysis to be subsequently performed. Readers familiar with the work of Carl Rogers will find similarities to Kaiser throughout this paper.[2]

Kaiser rejected any approach to the therapeutic practice that involved the therapist in making a match between the patient's thoughts and actions and a model of psychopathology. He further objected to imposing the results on the patient. He rejected any "working on" on or "working with" the patient wherein the therapist guides the patient in a specific predetermined direction.

Kaiser's ideas have always been exciting and powerful: He made an impression on Freud; he made an impression on Wilhelm Reich; he made an impression on Otto Fenichel; he made an impression on David Rapaport; he made an impression on Karl Menninger; he also made an impression on James Bugental, Irvin Yalom, David Shapiro, Louis Fierman, Alan Enelow and a host of others who became familiar with his body of work and studied with him in private seminars.

It is my position that the foundations of Kaiser's views on psychotherapy are based on the dynamics that operate in ordinary interactive structures. He was most likely unaware of these structures. Kaiser's explicit aim was to gain an understanding of the therapist's role during the therapeutic encounter. He wanted to know how the therapist paid attention to the patient: What did he do with that attention? He did not want to know why the patient came to have the neurotic symptoms he developed. Max Weber once commented that you do not have to be Caesar in order to know Caesar. Similarly, Kaiser's view was that a therapist did not need to know the underlying psychological mechanisms involved in the patient's pathology in order to treat the patient. Electronic circuit designers, for example, may not know exactly why electrons move through a wire, but even without that knowledge, they can perform miracles in creating electronic devices. Kaiser observed anomalies in patients' behaviors that are sometimes subtle and sometimes glaring. He called these anomalies (electron-like-entities), their *duplicity*.

It was his claim that therapeutic changes can take place by means of a technique of bringing patients' *duplicitous* behaviors to their attention. The patient's neurotic symptoms would progressively diminish and eventually disappear. By means of this process, over time, patients are cured.

Hellmuth Kaiser identified *duplicity* as the "universal symptom." Nowhere does he provide a clear definition. The locus of the universal symptom, the underlying dynamic, is in the communicative process between patient and therapist. Kaiser focused primarily on the therapist in this process.

This paper will examine two concepts introduced by Kaiser: *duplicity* and the *therapist's communicative attitude*. Unfortunately, one cannot read Kaiser's work and use the totality of his observations and illustrations as a primer for practicing his style of psychotherapy. Throughout his body of work, Kaiser provides a variety of illustrations of these concepts. These concepts do not apply to attributes of the patient, nor of the therapist. They apply to a therapist's approach to a patient's behavior and to the therapist's reaction to those behaviors. I offer an interpretation of Kaiser's concepts using, as a frame of reference, the flow of interaction: not only what the patient and therapist say and do, but also how their behaviors are part of a unique dynamic that emerges in the interactions between them.

Kaiser's Departure from Psychoanalysis

Kaiser's interest in psychotherapy began when he himself was a patient in psychoanalysis. Before he had any formal training, he wrote a psychoanalytic paper, "Kleist's Prinz von Hamburg" (Kaiser, 1930). Freud read it and sent Kaiser a flattering four-page, hand-written commentary.[3] A few years later, Freud interceded in Kaiser's behalf and helped him gain admission to the Berlin Psychoanalytic Institute. Kaiser became a psychoanalyst.

Because Freud's main interest was to develop a comprehensive theory of psychopathology, he did not detail a program for the practice of therapy. At first,

Kaiser attempted to fill that void within the framework of psychoanalysis. A number of intervening factors contributed to his taking a different path. Eventually he devoted himself exclusively to the understanding of the therapist's role in the therapeutic process.

Kaiser (1934) wrote a paper called, "Problem of Technique," where he began to map his version of an extension within psychoanalysis. This paper was not well received.[4] Subsequently, he no longer addressed psychoanalytic issues. His departure from psychoanalysis was also evident in the literary form he used to convey his point of view.

The last paper he wrote, "The Universal Symptom of the Psychoneuroses: A Search for the Conditions of Effective Psychotherapy,"[5] is written in the form of a pseudo-biographical novel. In it, the innovative and experimental therapist (designated as "G...")[6] explored a variety of simple strategies in communicating with his patient. Some changes were extremely subtle. For example, he changed the approach in the opening exchanges in the first few seconds the therapist spent with a new patient from what he had been taught in his psychoanalytic training. The results of these experiments lead to the development of a model for an effective psychotherapy. Included in his program are the following themes:

1. Nothing is required of the patient except his physical presence.
2. All responsibility for the outcome of therapy rests with the therapist.
3. There is no causal connection between the changes that take place in therapy and the topics discussed.
4. The therapist must always be psychologically available to the patient.
5. Psychotherapy is not an enterprise that directly solves practical problems.

In Kaiser's (1965) paper "Emergency,"[7] a second paper that departed from traditional academic form, Kaiser used the form of a seven-scene play. The play depicts a Kaiserian therapist who races to keep another therapist from committing suicide. The play is filled with suspense and melodrama and was designed to illustrate an important theme in Kaiser's work: Therapy can take place without the requirement that a patient cooperate.

In the play, this premise is pushed to the extreme: The wife of a severely depressed therapist convinces the Kaiserian therapist to accept her husband as a patient by becoming her husband's patient.[8] The husband becomes the unwitting patient. This impossible (as well as unethical) premise of the play was invented by Kaiser as a didactic device: He wanted to demonstrate some of the principles of his therapeutic techniques—without getting bogged down with theoretical explanations or justifications. One of the main attractions of this format is that his ideas are not clouded by academic jargon. The exposition of his ideas is clear, simple and makes good sense.

Problem: the Mystery in the Outcome of Psychotherapy

The "Universal Symptom…," chronicles the development of his therapeutic process. At one point, Kaiser (1965b) posed the rhetorical question: "From where does therapy derive its magic power?" The answer Kaiser gave was: "…it is located in the 'therapist's communicative attitude'."[9] His use of the term "magic" is jarring since Kaiser was a scientist as well as a clinician. He received his Ph.D. in mathematics and philosophy, before he became a psychoanalyst. His use of the term does not refer to slight-of-hand trickery. The use of the term "magic" calls attention to the magnitude of Kaiser's awe of the changes that take place <u>resulting</u> from psychotherapy. The term "magic" refers to a mystery in the connection between the application of a therapeutic technique and its beneficial results.

The phrase, *therapist's communicative attitude* suggests that, in the clinical setting, the thoughts expressed by the therapist are expected to have an effect on the patient. It is obvious that any changes would be achieved through communication. That interpretation is overly simplistic. For Kaiser, the *therapist's communicative attitude* denotes an intimate involvement with the patient and with his universal pathology, *duplicity*. For Kaiser, an essential part of a *therapist's communicative attitude* is the availability to react to the behaviors of the patient.[10]

The magic in the process of psychotherapy cannot be explained by understanding *duplicity* or the *therapist's communicative attitude*. No single event explains the magic of the changes that take place. The magic refers to the result of a series of processes triggered by the mutual reactions between patient and therapist.[11] Neither *duplicity* nor the *therapist's communicative attitude* exists outside the therapy session.

Illusive Aspects of Kaiser's Ideas

Kaiser was aware that he did not provide a clear description of his ideas. In his introduction to "Emergency," Kaiser (1965a), acknowledges his awareness of the vagueness in how he presents his ideas; those remarks apply to his concepts of *duplicity* and the *therapist's communicative attitude* as well.

The views [expressed in this paper, "Emergency"]…are my views. They are not easy to present or to transmit, not because they imply a complicated theory, but because they are simple where one expects the elaborate. When they are expressed in abstract terms, as a textbook would do, the reader is likely to miss their meaning, as if he had to decipher a melody from the grooves of a gramophone disk. (p. 172)

Kaiser presented his ideas about therapeutic methods indirectly. Purposefully. Kaiser was quite capable of doing otherwise,[12] but did not use the form of a scientific paper. The reason was that the phenomena he dealt with were ephemeral: the perception and reaction to anomalies in an on-going course of interaction that contain the simultaneous expression of two attitudes. These anomalies, because they occur during the on-going interaction, are fleeting. They can easily be missed.

Kaiser's ideas about this dialectic—the interplay between the attitudes that shape a patient's behaviors and the therapist's reactions to those behaviors, cannot be specified directly.

Duplicity and Reacting to *Duplicity*

The following is an imaginary speech by Freud. It was created by the author as an indirect means of looking at some of Kaiser's central ideas. In a more direct approach, each sentence in the speech would require an expansion into several pages or chapters. The speech also places Kaiser's work in historical perspective and raises some clinical issues:

> *Freud, in the 21st Century, mysteriously appeared at a psychological conference and addressed not just psychoanalysts, but therapists of every persuasion. He began by defending himself against various writers who besmirched his personal character. Their intention was to cast doubts on his intellectual achievements. It seemed that his speech had ended when he suddenly smiled in anticipation of the strange words he was about to utter. He took a deep breath, shook his head, and said:*
>
> "…Look, you paid too much attention to what I said and did not pay sufficient attention to what I did in the course of treating my patients–especially early on. At the outset, I was not concerned with rules and did not have many theories.
>
> I listened to my patients for hours and hours and allowed them to speak with very little interruption. Eventually I got to know what Wilhelm Reich called each person's "character."

On rare occasions, I noticed peculiarities in my patient's behavior that I had not anticipated: Sometimes, a patient would laugh in midstream of a sentence (it was not laughter that was in response to a joke); sometimes his words would assume a voice that was completely out of sync with his personality (timidity in the midst of anger, or proclamation of poverty when he had a sizable bank account), etc. The behaviors were bizarre—but not by reference to some model of ideal mental health. During those exceptional moments, my attention was attracted to what my patients did and not to an analysis of their neuroses.

Even my own behaviors at those moments were puzzling. I found myself laughing when the subject of a patient's talk was serious. My patients never found such laughter disrespectful. No disrespect was intended. At times, I offered caricatures of a patient's behaviors: 'You are talking as if you can't get off a speeding train fast enough;' or 'You sound as though you are a spy, but no one told you what you are supposed to be looking for.' I see now that those caricatures were metaphors capturing essential behavioral qualities.

Therapy-as-usual had been temporarily suspended.

These special instances were unique in other respects as well. My comments, which seemed so frivolous and incongruous when examined out of context, had an impact on patients and provided them with images of how their attitudes shaped their behaviors. During those moments, patients responded as if something very profound had been revealed. My bizarre comments, while essentially true, were valid only then and there.

I never wrote about these unusual experiences. It was not clear to me why these peculiar interchanges found their way into the therapy hour in the first place. Introspection was of no avail.

I described and analyzed a related group of unusual and puzzling behaviors in my Psychopathology of Everyday Life (Freud, 1965): "Slips of the tongue" and "the contagion of forgetfulness" are two examples. These unusual and unexpected behaviors were not noticed until I drew attention to them. In that book, I explained their connection to the subconscious.

The entire collection, of all the unusual behaviors, has a feature in common: The interactive context is an underlying factor.

Wilhelm Reich had a student, Hellmuth Kaiser, who turned his attention exclusively to these peculiarities. The events I noticed only infrequently, Kaiser found ubiquitous. The reason is that I was distracted by my zeal to search a patient's "materials" for evidence consistent with my theories and did not pay attention to the patient in his totality.

Kaiser's view of the therapist's role in therapy differed from my own.

I advocated analyzing the patient's pathology: In my view, the therapist guided the patient towards an understanding of his presenting symptoms as aspects of his pathology. When, for example, a patient gained insight into his pathology, this represented to me an improvement in his mental health. In contrast, Kaiser's position was that he had nothing to teach patients about themselves. When his patients expressed insights, he regarded these as no different from any other clinical material. He did not encourage his patients to gain an awareness of their pathology. What Kaiser did do was to point out to his patients the <u>simultaneous</u> presence of two <u>attitudes</u> exhibited in their behavior. This he called the patient's *duplicity.*

Kaiser observed that patients are never consciously aware of their *duplicity. Duplicity* is always invisible to the patient and only achieves a reality when it is reacted to and described by the therapist.

Another point of divergence between our viewpoints is that I considered the patient's cooperation an essential component of the curative process. In Kaiser's view, there was nothing the patient could do to accelerate his own treatment and no cooperation was required. Without requiring the patient's cooperation, in principal at least, it did not matter to Kaiser whether his patients were truthful or deceitful.

From Kaiser's perspective, the therapist was merely a catalyst: Changes in a patient's symptoms were the result of the cumulative experiences in the patient's communication with the therapist.

Freud paused, looked out at his audience, smiled, and his changed tone of voice signaled he understood their surprised reaction. He continued to smile as he said:

How strange it would feel to one of my patients if he were to enter into treatment with Kaiser. How strange it would be for the patient not to be asked to bring in recollections of dreams. How strange it would be for the patient not to be asked to speak with wanton abandon. How strange it would be for the patient not to collaboratively review, with meticulous care, a history that provided clues to lost memories of a traumatic past. How strange it would be for the patient not to view his thoughts and actions as symbolically connected to past events and relationships. How strange it would be for the patient to leave all the work of treatment in the hands of the therapist."

With those words, Freud suddenly disappeared.[13]

There are several unanswered questions posed by this fictitious speech: What are the anomalies in a patient's behavior? What is *duplicity*? How is Kaiser's idea of a *therapist's communicative attitude* different from other ideas of a therapist's attitude? How can a therapist be surprised by his own behaviors? How can therapy be anything but a <u>learning</u> experience for the patient?

Kaiser's perspective on therapy offers novel alternatives that are not direct answers to these questions.

The Interactive Context and Psychology

Kaiser shifted away from a focus on a patient's psychology (his psychopathology), towards a focus on the therapist and the way in which he attends the patient's behavior. Psychologists and others have been aware of the minute interplay and influence that actions and reactions have in the course of interaction.

Charles Darwin (1872) observed that the capacity to blush is a characteristic unique to the human species. Blushing reflects an inner psychological state. This reaction is involuntary and is publicly visible. Anna Freud (1946) noted that, in children, expressions of spontaneous laughter are involuntary and provide the analyst with an uncensored picture of the child's inner state of mind. Harry Stack Sullivan (1954) commented that schizophrenic patients sometimes experience the "eyes as the windows to the soul." They feel that others can have access to their innermost states of mind.

How are the experiences of blushing, of spontaneous laughter, and of piercing paranoid self-consciousness related to one another? Each is an illustration of a dramatic psychological reaction that is experienced or expressed by one individual <u>while in the presence</u> of another. Each occurs within an <u>on-going</u> course of interaction.[14]

Although not using the same terminology employed in this paper, the connection between psychological dynamics and the structures of ordinary interaction were noted by David Rapaport (1967) and by Frieda Fromm-Reichman (1950). Rapaport was aware of the differences between the therapeutic relationship and the interpersonal (interactive) relationship.[15] He made a distinction between two types of perspectives on the interplay between the individuals interacting in the clinical setting:

1. <u>analyst-analysand</u> (a perspective used in psychoanalysis)
2. <u>interactive relationship</u> (a perspective used in sociology)

The interactive context, the arena in which psychotherapy takes place, has a dynamic that is <u>not</u> part of, and therefore distinct from, Rapaport's concern with a psychoanalytic understanding of the relationship between the participants. Rapaport did not specify the details of that distinction and he did not elaborate on the interactive relationship.

Frieda Fromm-Reichman (1950) was aware that dynamics in <u>ordinary interactions</u> could interfere in the process of therapy. These dynamics can impinge on the behavior of the therapist when he interacts with his patient.[16] She was acutely aware of a natural, spontaneous and compelling tendency on the part of the therapist to search out problems from his own personal experiences when listening to problems presented by the patient:[17]

> What then are the basic requirements as to the personality and the professional abilities of a psychiatrist?...I would reply, 'The psychotherapist must be able to listen.' This does not appear to be a startling statement, but it is intended to be just that. To be able to listen and to gather information from another person...without reacting along the lines of one's own problems or experiences, of which one may be reminded...is an art of interpersonal exchange which few people are able to practice.... <u>The therapist must avoid reacting to patients' data in terms of his own life experience</u>.... [and] to concentrate upon listening to the patient. [Emphasis added] (Fromm-Reichman, 1950, p. 7)

The interactive relationship, a non-psychological relationship, has relevance within the clinical setting because the participants are engaged in social interaction. Neither Rapaport nor Reichman attribute any pathology to the interactive relationship. Whereas Rapaport was interested in the global aspect of the <u>interactive relationship</u>, Reichman was sensitive to a dynamic within such a relationship. Reichman points to a reflexive reaction that invariably takes place in the clinical setting because the therapist and patient are at the same time participants in ordinary social interaction. The structural rules that apply in ordinary conversation apply to the clinical setting as well. Social structures, like their psychological counterparts (attitudes) influence the minutest aspects of behavior.

Social Structures Shape Behaviors

The following sociological analysis of an interaction between a mother and her child is an example of a situation where an understanding of the words alone would miss a socially structured dynamic that surfaces only in the course of an on-going interaction. While the behaviors of the participants are influenced by social structures, the participants are not aware of the dynamics involved. Similar dynamics apply to the clinical setting:

This exchange takes place in an examining room of a doctor's office in a hospital:[18]

(Pause)

Mother: What do you say?
Child: Thank you.
When a mother says to her child: "What do you say?" it is not difficult to imagine that immediately preceding his mother's question, the child was doing nothing. There was a silence. It was a silence that belonged to the child. The mother, however, experienced a sense of urgency during the silence to do something. There was someone other than the child present—the doctor. She heard in the silence, an absence. Hearing an absence is not the same as hearing nothing. A silence in an interactive context is itself an action. Her son's action, the silence, had a coercive influence on her: It prompted her to ask her question. She reacted to the silence. Her reaction was not an elective act. She could not choose to do nothing. She was compelled to ask her question. It is not enough for the mother to know her child's repertoire of responses.

At that instant, in the course of the interaction, she executes a cultural imperative. Her orientation is to enforce social norms of politeness. Her behavior is a cultural instrument and she complies as if she were following a mandate to ask her question. The question she asks is not like asking for the time of day. Her question serves as our culture's device for teaching children abstract thought: to recognize specific instances as belonging to categories that are governed by the application of a rule. Her action, a reaction to her child's silence, instructs her child: "You need to recognize that this circumstance is typical for similar situations. You need to select an appropriate match from that collection of responses that you already know." The child's silence reflects that he failed to acknowledge in a culturally prescribed manner his appreciation in receiving something that qualifies as a gift [the doctor gave him a lollipop]. The mother is predisposed to react to her child's silence. She does this in compliance with her culture's expectations as his caretaker. Once the mother's question is posed to the child, the appropriate response, "Thank you" was made and correctly filled the void.

It is not incidental, but culturally axiomatic, that parents are charged with socializing their children. They are suited to do so not because they have read Dr. Spock, or Amy Vanderbilt. But they are particularly suited to preserve and perpetuate a culture's social norms because they are positioned to react to transgressions in the behavior of their children.

> This exchange could not take place without semantic understanding. This example illustrates structural dynamics within interactions: While a mother orients to issues of politeness, she is participating in a much larger cultural process–teaching abstract thinking. (Krakowski, 1968)

While the mother is enforcing politeness, her attention in executing this task is directed towards a narrow spectrum of the totality of the child's behavior. Similarly, Reichman focuses on a narrow range of a therapist's attention to a patient's behavior when she recommends that he exercise control over his natural inclinations as an ordinary conversant to not insert his own recollections during clinical exchanges.[19]

Kaiser's therapeutic recommendation was just the opposite. He advocated no restrictions in the natural flow of interaction with the patient.. He recommended sensitivity to the entirety of the interactions in the clinical setting. This is part of the *therapist's communicative attitude*. He urged that the therapist not interfere with his natural inclination to react to any aspect of the patient's behavior.[20] In short, he urged a therapist to be himself and not assume a role–that of a therapist.[21]

An Illustration of *Duplicity:* a Contrast in Affect

Duplicity refers to a duality. The selection of that term by Kaiser was unfortunate. It would have been preferable if Kaiser had selected a term from a different language: from French, "duplicite," or from German, "doppelzüngigkeit." Terms from a foreign language would not immediately bring to mind familiar psychological processes. Kaiser's use of the term does not refer to a malady. Kaiser's use of the term focuses on the therapist's sensitivity to duplicitous behaviors.[22]

The following is a clinical example of *duplicity*. It distinguishes between a perspective of a patient-and-his-problem vs. the perspective of the therapist and how he observes-the-patient's-behaviors. It will be used to illustrate how Kaiser's approach to the therapeutic process is unencumbered by analytic meanderings.

First, I will present a view that is contrary to Kaiser's approach. The materials are compiled from a series of the author's file notes.

"He smiled without knowing that he was smiling."[23] (Kaiser, 1965b, p. 90)

> In his therapy hour, a patient reported that the night before he had a bitter fight with his wife. The patient insisted he was right during the fight. He had ranted and raved in his efforts to set things right. There had been an injustice.
>
> He was clearly agitated as he recounted the events.
>
> As he delivered his narrative, there was an increase in the amplitude and pitch of his voice and in the rhythm of his speech. As the narrative proceeded, the therapist noticed a peculiar accompanying feature: Throughout the narrative, the patient wore a plastered smile. His smile was reminiscent of a father who was boasting that the home team had won the championship and his son was the star.
>
> The patient was genuinely surprised when the therapist pointed out the smile. Yet, it was as though the therapist's words fell on deaf ears: When the patient continued the narrative, the smile immediately returned.. (Krakowski, 2001)

The two affective components of the patient's behavior, the smile and the hostility in the narrative, are logically opposed to one another. Were the patient conscious of his smile, that awareness would undermine his insistence that he was right.

Yet the smile suggests that he <u>knows</u> something. It is obvious by watching and listening to the unfolding narrative, that the patient does <u>not know</u> what drives the smile.

To Know and Not to Know—a Problem and its Resolution

This juxtaposition of affects is puzzling. When the patient smiles throughout the course of a narrative filled with anger and is oblivious to the smile, it poses a putative paradox: There is something the patient both <u>knows</u> and <u>does not know</u> at the same time. How can anyone, at the same instant, both know and not know?[24]

First, I will present a conjectural exploration of the problem: The patient's pathology is at the center of the discussion. Then I will present a view of the same clinical situation: The therapist's posture is the center of discussion (a Kaiserian perspective).

From the point of view of the patient's perception of himself, this example poses a discrepancy in how he wishes he were viewed by others and constitutes a contrast in the image displayed in his behavior. One explanation is that the smile is prompted by the patient's <u>anticipation</u> that the therapist will react with surprise at his confrontational behavior in and out of the office. The patient may even feel a sense of triumph. From his viewpoint, his actions in the fight transformed an image of himself as someone with a mundane personality to someone with a more noble personality: He had stuck to his guns in the face of adversity. In his eyes, with his bold actions, he elevated the stature of the image of his character.

Another approach to understanding this circumstance is that his smile represents the outcome of the patient's juxtaposition of two contrasting images he has of himself: On the one hand, he sees himself as a reasonable, gentle and kind intellectual; on the other hand, he is aware that his exaggerated and volatile behavior paints a picture of him as a bully. As he delivers the narrative, he anticipates that the therapist will actively see him as a bully as well.[25]

Other viewpoints can easily be imagined that are equally plausible. Such accounts assume that the patient's reasoning is rational even if his behavior is not. Such accounts are speculative and require making theoretical assumptions. Such accounts are not based on observation.

It can be observed that the patient's attention is riveted to the fight. His dramatic re-creation revives the emotions he experienced during the fight, and this is dramatically displayed in the delivery of his narration. His presentation in the office seems to be theatrically orchestrated. It is unlikely that he was smiling in the heat of his dispute–but it is not impossible.[26] The smile surfaces the instant the narration begins and but does not stop upon completion of the narrative. The simultaneous appearance of the smile and the expression of anger are alien to him. It is as if an external influence intrudes upon him. The smile has a life of its own.

The paradox is an analytic construct. It is valid, but only under the condition that its components are composed of discrete abstract elements removed from the context in which they occurred.[27] The paradox involves two opposing ideations: The thoughts that lay claim to the patient's convictions that his anger is justified and the thoughts that evoke the patient's expression of apparent amusement. The narrative differs from a monologue, an entry in a diary or a report dictated into a recording device. The paradox <u>fails</u> to take into account that the narrative occurs in the presence of the therapist. The paradox consists of components that have been artificially removed from the interactive context in which they took place.

An examination of the component elements of the paradox, that more closely tracks the events as they transpired, reveals an important flaw in the formulation of the paradox: There is a difference between an ideation and an experience.

The first "know" contained in the paradox refers an <u>experience,</u> and not to an ideation. He does not "know" his <u>experience of the smile</u>. What he is not aware of is not something that he might be thinking, but something his body is doing. The patient reacts with what appears to be amusement and is not aware of his <u>experience of that reaction.</u>

This paradox overlooks a critical feature of language: The same terms in a language can be both precise and ambiguous. The paradox is dependent on the reader's tacit acquiescence <u>not to notice</u> that the meanings of the term "know" shifts from the first part of the formulation to the second. The first "know" implies an awareness of an <u>experience</u>. The second "know" refers to an <u>obligation</u> to know: He <u>should</u> know the object of the first "know." The first "know" refers to an analyst's claim about the presumed cognitions of the patient, and the second "know" refers to the patient's absence of an awareness of the analyst's claim. In the context in which the smile took place, the patient does not know that he <u>reacts to something in his environment</u>.[28]

The presence of the therapist affects the shape of the patient's behavior in ways that are unclear.[29] Independent of any specification of that influence, the paradox failed to take into account that the smile occurred while the patient was <u>talking to his therapist</u>.

The paradox is resolved! Or more correctly, within the flow of the clinical interaction, there is no paradox.

Push and Pull, and the Communicative Attitude

The discussion thus far has explored the patient's behaviors from an existential and phenomenological point of view. It has explored the patient's relationship to his behaviors, his attitudes, his experiences, his awareness, etc. The resolution of the paradox is a trivial triumph. The resolution of the paradox does not solve any practical or theoretical problems. Kaiser's work does not offer a means to solve paradoxes. Furthermore, within Kaiser's framework, paradoxes involving a patient's behavior are irrelevant.

A Kaiserian perspective focuses on the actions of the therapist. This clinical example will now be examined from that perspective.

Every therapist watches and listens. It is puzzling why this therapist did not see the smile from the outset. This therapist did not see the smile until the narrative was well under way.

Some therapists never see the smile!

In this and similar circumstances, the therapist's blindness to the smile does not reflect a shortcoming in his skills as a therapist. The blindness is induced in the therapist as a consequence of the behaviors of the patient. It is as if the patient engages in a strategy to distract the therapist. The patient's neurotic attitudes guide the course of his actions. Those attitudes are at work in innumerable ways—but they are not haphazard. With his narrative, the patient seduces the therapist into surrendering his attention to the drama of the story. The narrative is told so as to convey a sense of urgency. The patient gives the impression that his interest is singular and focused. The narrative is designed to get the therapist to side with him and to help find a solution to his problem. The patient's actions are geared not only to have the therapist agree that his claims in the fight were justified, but they are also geared to get the therapist to feel sorry for him. The patient's narrative is delivered in such a fashion so as to gain a sympathetic ally. His narrative is delivered with a missionary-like zeal.

A friendship has developed over the course of their therapeutic contact. The therapist, because of the patient's underlying efforts, vacillates between his feelings of friendship towards the patient and his professional responsibility to cure him. Consequently, the therapist is vulnerable. The narrative cloaks a plea for help. The therapist is only human. He succumbs. At the instant he sympathizes with the patient's predicament, he is blinded to the existence of the smile (perhaps no differently than the patient is blinded to his own smile). Throughout the narrative, not only is the patient upset with his wife, but he is also, at the same time, outraged that he is a victim of her abuse. The successfully seduced and sympathetic therapist will immediately contemplate remedies. If the patient succeeds in winning him over, the therapist acts as a friend. At the point the therapist acts as a friend, the patient has succeeded in distracting the therapist.[30] Unwittingly, the patient impedes progress in his own treatment.

What choices are available to the therapist as an alternative to acting like a friend? What does the cure consist of?[31]

1. The therapeutic cure is not to stop the patient from smiling. To smile in a circumstance such as this is not a malady. The smile accompanies the malady.
2. The therapeutic cure is not to promote an attitude where the patient would feel better about this fight nor to persuade him to stop fighting. Even if the therapist had the power to do so, this path might lead the patient to become overly placid and at the extreme, vegetative. It is not the goal of therapy to break his spirit.[32]
3. The therapeutic cure is not to persuade him to stay in the marriage, nor to leave it. It is not the goal of therapy to become a surrogate decision-maker.[33]

A Kaiserian perspective would examine the therapist's role in this interaction.

When Kaiser's idea of a *therapist's communicative attitude* is applied to this clinical example:

1. It does not matter that there is something the patient <u>knows and does not know</u> <u>at the same time</u>.

2. It does not matter <u>why</u> the patient has the problems he presents as his complaints.

Kaiser's approach does not require that the therapist be able to explain or understand the nature of the "malady." In Kaiser's approach, more important than anything else (from a practical standpoint of the therapeutic process), is that the therapist <u>not</u> get distracted by the patient's behavior. When the therapist pays attention to the totality of a patient's behavior and is mindful of the patient's alternative attitudinal possibilities, this will increase the possibility to notice the smile.

When the therapist sees the smile, he assumes a posture in which he is disattentively attentive[34] to the patient's behavior. He is both an active and a passive agent in that setting. To the extent that he is attentive, he is a co-participant in the interaction with the patient. To the extent that he is disattentive, he is a passive witness to the variety of events before him and is thereby available to react to those behaviors.[35] He must do both, simultaneously: assume a posture that is attentive and disattentive.

Kaiser's therapeutic approach does not focus on <u>interpreting</u> or <u>understanding</u> the content, issues, or specific concerns of the patient. Instead, his therapeutic approach views the totality of the patient's behavior. The approach is optimally designed to allow the therapist to be available to react to <u>any</u> aspect of the patient's behavior. This is the *therapist's communicative attitude.* The <u>communicative attitude</u> does not attempt to get the patient to understand, to accept or to ignore the smile.

The act of pointing out the smile, pointing out the patient's *duplicity*, is the curative agent.

A Second Illustration of *Duplicity*: The Shape of Behavior

It should not be assumed that because the above example of *duplicity* involved opposite affects that this is always the case. Opposite affects are but one form of expression of *duplicity* and not the most prevalent nor necessarily the most interesting. *Duplicity* permeates every therapy session. It is not immediately apparent. The smile, for example, was not immediately apparent. When the therapist, like the mother who notices the child's silence, notices and reacts to the patient's *duplicity*, he may, like the mother, feel an urge (culturally speaking), to point it out to the patient.

In the following excerpt from a therapy session, there is an example of *duplicity*. This therapist, Carl Rogers, had never heard of Kaiser.

Rogers was the first psychologist who published the entirety of his therapy sessions verbatim. The following fragment is from Rogers' (1942) <u>Counseling and Psychotherapy</u>:

C= counselor [therapist] S=subject [client]
1. C: Have you worried a lot about this matter of writing home?
2. S: About this? Well, yes, because it is going to be a pretty difficult proposition to put it across. I have not got any idea of what action they are going to take.
3. C: You sound as though you feel a little bit like a prisoner before the bar.
4. S: (Laugh) That's just about it. (p.136)

The therapist's[36] response in line three to the patient's remarks in line two is a departure from the style of interaction that transpired before and after this exchange. The therapist makes an observation in line three that takes the totality of the patient's behavior into account. The therapist's remarks differ from a variety of conventional possible responses: It does not contain an interpretation of the content of the patient's statement; it does not contain a connection to the patient's prior traumatic history; it does not contain advice; it does not contain a perspective of the patient by reference to psychopathology, etc.

If a word-for-word and line-by-line search were conducted on this fragment, *duplicity* would not jump off the page. Nevertheless, to the therapist in that exchange, the observation he made in his reaction to the patient's behavior is consistent with Kaiser's sense of *duplicity*.

While interacting with the patient, the therapist noticed a combination of elements that led to his impression that the patient was excessively formal. That impression may derive from the manner in which the patient expressed himself: the shape of his delivery, as well as the content of his response to the therapist's question. In combination, these components conveyed a sense of excessive formality.[37] The disparity between how his attitudes shape his verbal expression and the content of that expression is his *duplicity*. The therapist points to an anomaly in the patient's behavior: He speaks with an excessive formality and at the same time does not recognize that formality.

The relationship between the patient and his anticipated audience is that of a son speaking to his parent. By pointing to a formality in his mannerism, the therapist is not educating the patient. More importantly, in the therapist's act of pointing to a formality, the therapist is not being judgmental or directive.

This therapist's remarks were inconsistent with his announced model of psychotherapy as described in the first part of his book.[38] The comments he made to the patient at this particular instant fell outside that paradigm. At this instant, the therapist let his guard down and failed to censor his thoughts in accordance with his own theoretical aims.

The *duplicity* in this fragment differs from the smile-anger example in that it is not a juxtaposition of two opposite modes of affect. It is similar to the smile-anger example in that it illustrates how coexisting attitudes shape a patient's behavior.

Concluding Remarks

Kaiser's thinking was not only novel, it was also bold. He sought to enlarge the understanding of the therapist's function in the process of psychotherapy. Kaiser's illustrations of *duplicity* throughout his work do not define *duplicity*. The illustrations sensitize the reader to the nature of the phenomenon.[39]

The patient in therapy always creates the impression that he has a singular focus (even when he expresses an awareness of confusion). His *duplicitous* behaviors betray the presence of alternate thought structures. When the patient's misdirection of the therapist's attention is sufficiently effective, the *duplicity* remains unnoticed by the therapist and the neurotic symptoms remain intact. *Duplicity* does not reside in the patient. *Duplicity* lies in the fabric of the patient's behavior. The nap of that fabric is only accessible to the therapist and only at the instant in which it is expressed.

The beneficial outcome of the process of therapy is brought about, in part, by the *therapist's communicative attitude*. There are additional components that have not been broached in this paper. One such component has to do with the reaction by the patient to the therapist's reaction: The patient does not merely understand the therapist, he reacts to the therapist. The mystery and magic in the therapeutic process is the result of a mutual interplay of reactions.[40]

The elusive nature of the therapeutic process remains: Something in their interaction ensures that *duplicity* will remain unnoticed, and at the same time, something in their interaction prompts the therapist to notice *duplicity*. The patient perpetually engages in actions that misdirect the attention of the therapist: This is, in part the universal symptom—the *duplicity*. The *therapist's communicative attitude* is, in part, an attempt at averting that misdirective work in a non-self-conscious and effortless manner.[41]

The locus of *duplicity* and the locus of the *therapist's communicative attitude* is the interactive context.

Jerry Krakowski, is a sociologist who received his degrees from UCLA. He holds an Advancement to Candidacy degree. A student of Harvey Sacks at both UCLA and UCI, he has a continuing interest in Conversation Analysis. He is currently pursuing an expansion of his ideas of Kaiser's work and analyzing video and audio tapes of Carl Rogers.

REFERENCES

Adato, A. (1980). 'Occasionality' as a constituent feature of the known-in-common character of Topics. *Human Studies, 3*(1), 47-64.

Austin, J. L. (1962). *How to do things with words.* Cambridge, Massachusetts: Harvard University Press.

Darwin, C. (1872). *The Expressions of the emotions in man and animals.* New York: Appleton and Company.

Fenichel, O. (1953). *Collected papers of Otto Fenichel.* New York: Norton.

Fierman, L. B. (Ed.). (1965). *Effective Psychotherapy: The contributions of Hellmuth Kaiser.* New York: The Free Press.

Fierman, L. B. (1997). *The therapist is the therapy.* Northvale, New Jersey: Jason Aronson.

Fierman, L. B. (2002). *Freeing the human spirit.* Nevada City: Blue Dolphin Publishing.

Freud, A. (1946). *The ego and the mechanisms of defense.* New York: International Universities.

Freud, S. (1965). *Psychopathology of everyday life,* New York: W. W. Norton.

Fromm-Reichmann, F. (1950). *Principles of intensive psychotherapy.* Chicago: The University of Chicago Press.

Gill, M. M. (1967). *The collected papers of David Rapaport.* New York: Basic Books.

Greening, T., & Krakowski, J. (2002). Comparison of Carl Rogers and Hellmuth Kaiser. In *Carl Rogers Centennial.* Symposium conducted at the meeting of the Open Space, La Jolla, California.

Kafka, F. (1964). *The trial.* New York: The Modern Library. (Original work published 1937 Alfred A. Knopf Inc.).

Kaiser, H. (1930). Kleist's Prinz von Homburg. *Imago,* 16, 119-137.

Kaiser, H. (1931). Franz Kafka's Inferno: Eine psychologische Deutung seiner Strafphantasie. *Imago, 1931,* 53-61.

Kaiser, H. (1934). Probleme der technik. *Internationale Zeitschrift fur Psychoanalyse,* 20, 490-522.

Kaiser, H. (1955). *Seminar: "Wolfgang Lederer and the Comfort of Pseudoscience in Psychotherapy"* (transcript.) Retrieved from   http://www.hellmuthkaiser.org.

Kaiser, H. (1965a). Emergency. In L. B. Fierman (Ed.), *Effective psychotherapy: The contributions of Hellmuth Kaiser* (pp. 172-202). New York: The Free

Press. (Original work: Kaiser, H. (1962). Emergency. *Psychiatry, 25*, 97-118.)

Kaiser, H. (1965b) The Universal Symptom of the Psychoneurosis: A Search for the Conditions of Effective Psychotherapy. In L. B. Fierman (Ed.), *Effective Psychotherapy: The contributions of Hellmuth Kaiser* (pp. 14-171). New York: The Free Press.

Kaiser, H. (1972). Kafka's fantasy of punishment. In Corngold, S. (Ed.), *The Metamorphosis* (pp. 147-156). New York: Bantam Books.

Krakowski, J. (1968). *"What do you say?": Socialization of children.* Paper presented at the annual meeting of the American Sociological Association, Hawaii, and UCLA.

Krakowski, J. (1972). *Universals in the culture of highly functional mentally retarded persons.* Unpublished manuscript, Illinois Pediatric Institute.

Krakowski, J. (2000). *The placement of laughter in the course of talk.* Unpublished manuscript.

Krakowski, J. (2001). Author's personal files.

Reich, W. (1972). *Character analysis* (3rd ed.) New York: Farrar, Straus and Giroux. (Original work published 1933).

Rochman, J. (1999). *The therapeutic relationship.* Paper presented at the meeting of the Center for Effective Psychotherapy, Didi Hirsch Mental Health Center.

Rogers, C. R. (1942). *Counseling and psychotherapy.* New York: Houghton Mifflin Company.

Rogers, C. R. (1961). *On becoming a person.* Boston: Houghton Mifflin Company.

Sacks, H. (1992). *Lectures on conversation (I).* Oxford UK and Cambridge USA: Blackwell.

Sartre, J. (1956). *Being and nothingness.* New York: Philosophical Library.

Schafer, R. (1992). *Retelling a life.* New York: Basic Books Inc.

Shapiro, D. (1965). *Neurotic styles.* New York, London: Basic Books.

Shapiro, D. (1981). *Autonomy and rigid character.* New York: Basic Books Inc.

Shapiro, D. (1989). *Psychotherapy of Neurotic Character.* New York: Basic Books Inc.

Shapiro, D. (2000). *Dynamics of character.* New York: Basic Books.

Stack Sullivan, H. (1954). *The psychiatric interview.* New York: W. W. Norton and Company Inc.

Yalom, I. (2002). *The gift of therapy: An open letter to a new generation of therapists and patients.* New York: Harper Collins.

ENDNOTES

[1] Reich (1972).

[2] Two presentations making a comparison between Rogers and Kaiser were made at a single "Open Space" session of the Carl Rogers Centennial, La Jolla, July 2002: Fierman, L. (2002), and Greening, T. and Krakowski, J. (2002).

[3] See forward by Enelow in L. Fierman, (Ed.), (1965).

[4] See Reich (1972), p. 310. See Fenichel (1953)

[5] Kaiser in L. Fierman, (Ed.), (1965).

[6] He borrows from Kafka's (1964) The Trial, and uses the same style of a single-letter referent for the main character.

[7] Fierman, L. Ed.) (1965).

[8] Irvin Yalom (2002) in his book, The Gift of Therapy, has a chapter devoted to how patients bring about change in their therapists. Kaiser's "Emergency" is listed as one example. As a technical matter, the Kaiserian therapist in the play was never the patient—he only pretended to be the patient. Fierman (2002) has suggested that the reason that three therapists Kaiser, Rogers and Lomas, developed a posture of non-directive therapy is because their patients influenced them to do so.

[9] Kaiser, H. (1965b) p.162

[10] His thoughts and actions are a reflection of his reactions.

[11] See footnote 40

[12] Kaiser (1930, 1931) wrote several psychoanalytic papers that were published before he became a psychoanalyst. Kaiser (1931) also wrote a lengthy psychoanalytic paper examining various segments of the writing of Franz Kafka. A small segment appears in Stanley Corngold's (1972) translation of Kafka's (1964) Metamorphosis.

[13] The ideas contained in the scenario regarding Freud's early approach to patients have been expressed in Kaiser's writings and seminars. A transcript of a seminar given by Hellmuth Kaiser (1955) is available on the Internet. While it deals primarily with the topic of Wolfgang Lederer, it contains some of Kaiser's thoughts on Freud and Freud's early work as a therapist.

[14] Sometimes the mere potential for interaction can be sufficient to trigger these reactions.

[15] Rapaport (1967) states:

> If I investigate the relationship of two people, an interpersonal relationship, with a certain method, it is quite possible that the method that I adopt will tell me nothing about the interpersonal relationship. Or it may tell me only some-

thing about it...the interpersonal issue...[about the] patient and doctor–is also a basis for conceptualization. It is a difficult situation which leads to many complexities. (p.196)

[16] See Sacks, H. (1992) p.259 for a discussion of this passage by Frieda Fromm-Reichman.

[17] The range of recollections can be extended to include jokes, reminiscences, etc.

[18] Dr. Barbara Korsch at Children's Hospital of Los Angeles kindly provided the author with tape-recorded interviews between doctors and parents with their children. Dr. Barbara Korsch was principal investigator in a variety of studies dealing with doctor-patient communication. Krakowski, J. (1968) reported his analysis of a mother/child relationship.

[19] See Adato, A. (1980). In personal communication, Adato expressed that "conversants routinely draw from the immediate occasion such events and features of it which provide for the sense of topicality, of what they're talking about". Adato shows how topics, similar to a mother's attentiveness to a silence, are intimately linked to the local setting–within the flow of natural conversation. His data consisted of a series of tape-recorded lunchroom conversations at a white-collar business.

[20] He neither prescribed nor restricted a code of conduct for the therapist. Here is another similarity between how Hellmuth Kaiser and Carl Rogers may have practiced therapy.

[21] The formulation: "be yourself," has a familiar ring in contemporary psychotherapy, particularly humanistic psychology. What is of interest is not merely the similarity between a variety of formulations, but the path that is taken in arriving at each of the formulations.

[22] The relationship between the two (or more) attitudes is not fixed: They may or may not be contrasting; They may or may not be in conflict with one another; They may or may not derive from one another, etc. Their interrelationship may never be clear. That understanding is irrelevant to a course of treatment.

[23] In Kaiser's (1965b) monograph, "Universal Symptom....," the narrator made this observation about "G..." The quoted remark refers to behavior of the therapist. The quote is interesting because it suggests that while Kaiser did not address clinical materials from the perspective employed in this paper, he seems to have made observations of his own clinical experience similar to those discussed in this paper: smiling and, in a special way, not being aware of smiling.

[24] Sartre (1956) confronted a similar question in his philosophical investigations that resembles the paradox of the smile. However, Sartre was occupied with investigations of perceptions of reality. He was interested in the question of what the individual simultaneously knows and does not know as an aspect of social, political and moral consciousness. His position was that when the individual does not

<u>know</u> what he <u>should know</u>, this was an instance of "bad faith" (self-deception). Sartre does <u>not</u> examine behavior in the course of an <u>interactive process.</u> His discussion of a paradox, though similar in its wording to the issues under discussion in this paper, does not apply. For a psychological examination of this issue, see Shapiro (2000) and his treatment of "self-deception."

Shapiro (1989, p. 74) describes a similar clinical example that I use here. Whereas his aim was to show what a patient "knows," the present aim, as will be developed shortly, is to examine how the therapist notices the smile, and thereby examining what the therapist "knows."

[25] By depicting himself as a bully, the patient seems to disregard the negative view he projects of himself. This is a common feature in a patient's interaction with his therapist. Nevertheless, there may be broader sociological and psychological implications to exposing oneself in an unfavorable light and <u>not being aware of it</u>. The patient's attention is focused towards convincing the therapist of the correctness of his position and he is not concerned about the possibility of making unfavorable impressions. The following illustration is offered to point to a similarity of this phenomenon to materials totally unrelated in every other respect.

In field observations by Krakowski, J. (1972), of behaviors in a mental retardation facility, one of the residents complained about another resident: "Tommy said 'fuck'." The resident did not avoid the use of the expletive, even when that usage could reflect badly on him. The resident used the word without regard that in his own action, by repeating the socially offensive word, he was committing the same transgression as the offending resident. Similarly, the patient in the present example did not avoid the possibility of making a negative impression in reporting his bully-like behavior.

[26] There is no reason to assume that the same dynamics that operate to conceal his self-awareness of the existence of the smile during the course of delivering his narrative were not also operative in the course of the fight. If he did smile during the fight, he would not be aware of his smile unless it was pointed out by someone else.

[27] Natural language philosophers and linguists examine utterances in isolation of the interactive context. For example, J. L. Austin's (1962) conception of words-as-actions, "performatives," he recognizes the significance of a social environment but only in so far as others are witnesses. Harvey Sacks (1992) treats action exclusively as having interactive consequences. *Duplicity*, as it is treated within this paper, is examined as a phenomenon within an interactive context.

[28] There are classes of behaviors that result from a reaction to a process of self-monitoring of one's own thoughts. Within a clinical setting, a patient may react to his own thoughts, impressions, behaviors, and attitudes in the same way that he reacts to the behaviors of the therapist. When the patient reacts to himself, he

reacts to his immediately preceding thoughts as if they were expression by another (not necessarily that of the therapist). For example, an insanely jealous teenager bitterly complained about his girlfriend. He was convinced that she is imminently on the verge of committing infidelity: "She has done it t-hhh-hhhe-hhhhe-wice already." He laughs uncontrollably as he says these words. He recognizes in that instant in which he was making a strong case for her frequent transgressions, that he has fudged in his calculation: she had "cheated" on her previous boyfriend, which made their present relationship with one another possible. He discovers while talking to the therapist that this prior transgression should not have counted against her. He identified her incorrectly as a frequent offender. He realizes that he was prejudicial in concluding that she was a frequent offender (he begins his statement that she had committed infidelity three times already). His conclusion that he was justified in his feelings of jealousy turns out, as he hears himself, to be based on a miscalculation. His laughter in the midst of his own talk was his reaction to the sudden awareness that his jealousy was objectively unfounded. The therapist's presence was the catalyst.

29 Roy Schafer (1992) makes a distinction between clinical and theoretical analysis: "...there is all the difference in the world between clinical and applied psychoanalysis for, in applied analysis, 'there is no patient to talk back.'" (p.174). This remark recognizes the potency of an interactive process.

30 David Shapiro (1989) has discussed the mechanism by which neurosis is self-preserving.

31 Carl Rogers (1961, p. 32) used the term "cure" as well, although he later replaced it with "personal growth."

32 Pharmacologists search for thresholds that fall short of inducing a vegetative state–particularly in institutional settings.

33 By definition, any non-directive therapy will have as an ideal not to interfere. Practical remedies are implicitly regarded as exempt. In a Kaiserian approach, practical remedies to problems fall outside of a concern with the anomalous shape of a patient's behaviors. The therapist's communicative attitude does not encourage a collaborative relationship between therapist and patient where the therapist is engaged in practical problem solving.

34 Jerry Rochman (1999), a psychologist who has for many years explored various aspects of Kaiser's thoughts, uses the phrase: "relaxed attention." This phrase captures the methodological ideal in anthropology of the non-participant observer. In that capacity the therapist is unobtrusive, while at the same time an observer. His discussion stimulated some of the thoughts in this paper.

35 At the instant the therapist sees the smile, he is empathic to the patient's attitude that produced the smile and not just the smile. Understanding, in this context, does not mean that the therapist needs to know the source of the smile.

[36] The terms "therapist" for "counselor," and "patient" for "client" are treated here interchangeably without intending any disrespect for the reasons that those terms are used in their original context.

[37] Heisenberg's Uncertainty Principle suggests that the measuring instrument may itself affect the resulting measurement. Had the question in this fragment not been posed by the therapist, the thoughts as they are expressed by the patient may not have occurred to the patient. The character of excessive formality in the patient's response may be the byproduct of responding to an unexpected question and not the anticipation of talking to his parents. This reasoning argues against this example as an instance of *duplicity*. Rogers, C. (1942 p. 137) comments on this very problem of the question he asks in this fragment. A Kaiserian therapist rarely asks such questions and Rogers asks such questions very infrequently. The discussions of materials in this paper are designed to illustrate, not to prove.

[38] In an annotative comment to this fragment, Rogers, C. (1942) is critical that the therapist was distracted from an ideal theoretical frame of reference as to how the interview should have been conducted. He singles out the same lines of text in this fragment as an instance in which the therapist had failed to adhere to the agenda of getting at the patient's feelings: "Only once is there any evidence that the counselor changes the train of Paul's [the client's] thought and feeling…to which Paul replies, 'About this?' showing that he has been thinking about something else." (p.137)

The comment in the annotation indicates that if he had had control over what he said in the interview, he would not have made this remark. To the extent that the therapist made a remark that he wished he had not made, this might suggest that in this instance, at least, the therapist had felt "culturally" (as that term is used in the context of this paper) compelled to make the remark.

[39] Fierman, in personal communication, expressed that Kaiser, towards the end of his career, dispensed with all concerns of *duplicity* and stressed instead a relationship of "communicative intimacy." Communicative intimacy is discussed in his book The Therapist is the Therapy, Fierman, L. (1997). The therapist's reaction to the patient's *duplicity*, as it has been presented in this paper is not an end in itself. It is only one component in the overall framework of Kaiser's therapeutic technique. In that overall framework, the therapist reacts to the patient in a seamless, effortless and non-directive manner. There is at least one other component that is not examined in this paper: the patient's reactions to the therapist's reaction. In the reaction of the patient to the therapist, it would seem that there is nothing in the therapist's behavior that would be unavailable to the patient; there is nothing the therapist needs to do other than be himself. Examining *duplicity*

and the *therapist's communicative attitude* is only a first step. A more detailed discussion lies outside the scope of this paper.

[40] The ideal therapeutic dynamic takes place when the therapist reacts to the patient's *duplicity* and the patient reacts to the therapist's reaction to his *duplicity* [See footnote 39]. The Rogers' excerpt may arguably contain an example of the patient's reaction to the therapist's reaction: his laughter in line 4. The claim that the laughter serves such a function is, from an analytic point of view, only tentative: It requires an analysis of laughter as a social structure in the course of interaction.

[41] See in particular Shapiro's (1989) Psychotherapy of Neurotic Character for his discussion about the therapist's experience in psychotherapy.

To Release the Spirit

Graham Harris

When asked to write a chapter for this book, I thought: why me, I am not a ther-apist or a professional psychologist or an academic. However, after some thought I decided to write about my 'lived inquiry', my journey and experiences with the Person Centred Approach. For me, The Person Centred Approach is merely as the name implies, an approach, nothing more; nothing less. It is an attitude of mind from which my thoughts and actions arise. It is a 'way of being'. (Rogers, 1980). A way of being that leads an individual to increased autonomy and psy-chological and spiritual growth. In other words: 'To become everything one is capable of becoming' (Maslow 1970).

It started some 15 years ago when I came across A Way of Being. I was pro-foundly struck by :

1. the frankness and honesty that changing oneself and/or another cannot be learned from books or training. It has to be a relationship. (Rogers 1954)
2. the energy that Rogers expounded 'for the development of creative, adap-tive, autonomous persons.' (Rogers 1954)
3. the paradox of its simplicity yet complexity. Simple in that to change; all I had to do was concentrate on myself and hold the three principles of empa-thy, unconditional positive regard and congruence. Complex in that I first had to understand what these three tenets were and meant. I guess my jour-ney thus far has been in this understanding.

Unconditional positive regard (upr), the act of entering mine and another's world with love and without judgement, appeared, at first, to be so easy, but the depth and subtlety of this statement has gradually hit me. It is relatively easy to deceive myself that I am showing upr and being empathetic but deep down I realise that really I want others to act and be like me. Rogers stated in his lecture to Oberlin College in 1954: "How can I provide a relationship, with myself, which I may use for my own personal growth."

The answer, for me, is through unconditional love. The ability to let go of the 'I' to become egoless and focus on the moment. In other words; 'I' is often used in the form of arrogance. What 'I' did......., what 'I' am saying....... etc implying that 'I' alone am right. This has the result of believing that there is only one way, one right answer and although we feel so important it has the net result of making us weak. Taking away our natural power of unconditionality and applying conditionality. A good test of whether you are managing to maintain your stance of upr is when someone challenges your actions or is disrespectful in some form or another. What is your reaction? Do you immediately feel hurt or insulted? The point is it is not what you think but what you feel. Many of us have learned to maintain our composure when delivered an unpleasant or unacceptable comment or experience, but what happens inside? It is our feelings that get transmitted to others, so, for me, having upr means not to react in any way whatsoever. Without a trace of feeling as well as thought. In my life I have only known three people who have this ability of giving unconditional love all the time. All are Indian and all are part of an organisation called the Brahma Kumaris. I realise that when I am in their company I feel special. I can feel the unconditionality. I feel they are focussed only on me and nothing I can say or do will change their acceptance of me.

The growth started when I had the courage to ask myself the question: who am I really? What is my natural state? Am I this mixed up bag of repression, suppression, habits and behaviours or am I something more than this? As I pondered this question I began to realise that I was naturally a loving, happy, peaceful person. As Rogers stated (1981),

> "members of the human species...are essentially constructive in their fundamental nature, but damaged by their experiences."

In the same way as Rogers recounted his early experience in his paper to Association of Humanistic Psychology in Honolulu in 1972 I had to learn to:

> "follow (my natural self's) lead rather than (my social self). I just had to listen instead of trying to nudge (myself) toward a diagnostic understanding that I had already reached."

I had to learn to respect and trust myself and my ability; to explore and understand myself. Learn to accept that I am naturally a good person, I am naturally loving and peaceful. If I truly believe in the actualising tendency then I can grow and develop. I can deal with myself unconditionally.

Over the years I have come to understand upr as the place where my thoughts, feelings, words and actions are synchronised. A place where I find that I am totally immersed in the relationship with another and where the words I use are very accurate and appear automatically. A place where I can feel a closeness which is natural and doesn't come for any particular reason. A place which can be experienced individually, one to one or when a member of a group. When I am in the state of upr I am also empathetic and congruent Like Mearns (1994), I too have come to the conclusion that the three tenets are inseparable, otherwise they can be used and manipulated as techniques that can be applied as and when required. I believe Rogers did not use them as techniques but reported on what he experienced. My feeling is that it doesn't matter where you start, whether you feel empathy is the key, upr or congruence because they are so interlinked, they will all take you to the same place. They are all approaches to life rather than techniques to be professionally applied. As Bozarth stated:

"The Person Centred Approach does not fit into the Cartesian logical approach of cause and effect but is more akin to a Systemic approach, where everything is interdependent".

So unconditional positive regard is a way of life that enables us to be at one with another and be totally in the now. However, in my experience I only achieve this when I am in 'feeling' mode rather than 'intellectual or thinking' mode. If this is the same for others then Rogers must be suggesting that not only is upr the focus from which all other tenets come but that the Person Centred Approach is an approach to run our lives by not a way to 'fix' or change others. To 'fix' must imply that there is a dominant or correct form of behaviour, a one right answer to which all must fit and those who are 'ill' or 'not right' are in need of repair. This surely is conditional positive regard. 'Fixing' others has the potential of leading to 'appalling consequences' (Rogers 1980) i.e. pulling people away from their natural self.

To achieve this state of upr, I found silence very powerful. Not an enforced silence of not talking but a quietness within where I can listen to myself with acceptance. Silence enables me to know myself and understand what is going on. A silence that is akin to real peace. A silence that is judged not in words but in feelings. For me the answer to my growth and development lies in this language of feelings. The more silent I become the more I become in tune with my natural self, my intuition or whatever you want to call it. So unconditionality is a place within me where I can just be. No doing, no pressure to perform a task, no pressure to be accepted by others, but to be my natural, peaceful, loving, happy self. Sometimes I notice that I am not that quiet, I am not in tune with myself but subtly I spend time doing or preparing to do or in criticising mine or others actions. When I am in this space of being seduced by my thoughts then I am not healing myself and I definitely cannot listen to others. For me silence is more than not talking, it is the place where I am at one with myself, where I am at one with nature. A feeling of being connected with the universe, being connected with my true self.

What stops me from achieving this? That well known avoidance phrase 'I don't have the time.' This is another of Rogers' paradoxes. To heal myself I have to allocate time and energy but in a stressful world of work, family, hobbies etc. my belief is I don't have the time to sit in the quiet with me. I see it as a waste of time. Whilst sitting alone I could be doing something, I ought to be doing something, I should be doing something.

I have come to realise that these words are the 'cripplers' the words that disable, undermine and impair my progress. Ought, should and must. I realised that as I used these words I was subtly suggesting that there was something or someone out there who had the answer. Then I realised that whenever I used ought, should or must to myself or others I was full of my own self importance. I was postulating how others needed to behave. How could I possibly know what others needed to do, I was not in their shoes I have no experience of their lives and yet I felt the need to pontificate on their behaviour. Actually, the bottom line is, Rogers is teaching us to accept others where they are and just listen. In their talking they will come to a place where they understand where and what they are doing. The same applies to me, all I have to do is listen to myself. In the silence just sit and listen and I will realise how far away from my natural state of love and peace I really am.

In this space I realised I can choose the route for my development. Either, I can go down the road of identifying all my defects and make effort to improve them one by one or I can come from the natural place and notice when I am not being congruent. I started by attempting to fix all my defects and after a while realised that this was very debilitating. Firstly, I was always dealing with the negative with the result I was always tired and felt depressed. Then I became aware that all the negatives or most of them came from past behaviour and I could do nothing about them. They had gone and were finished. Whatever I said to myself whatever I did I could not change the outcome so why was I worried about it? If I had upset anyone by my past behaviour then as sorry as I may feel now I could do nothing to make it right. It was done in those circumstances and as much as I wish I could change the circumstances I couldn't: the time had gone. So a major learning for me was to accept that the world of living was like the world of writing. When a sentence is finished apply a full stop and start again. I needed to accept this as a major tenet in my life; when an incident is over it is over I need to apply a full stop and move on. It doesn't mean that I don't have responsibility for my actions quite the opposite, but it does mean I can carry on with my life, my journey, my process. The aim, after all, is progressive movement, the will to keep growing, as Rogers stated, the main intention of a human being is the actualising tendency. The ability to grow. When I spend my time dwelling on the past I find I totally disempower myself.

What keeps me dwelling on the past? Fear. Fear is like a ghost. When it enters my mind it starts as a small thing, but it weakens me so much, so much that I am left with no energy, no enthusiasm and no power. Fear doesn't allow me to acknowledge my real self. Silence and the understanding of who I really am enables me to forget what has passed and stop dwelling in the past. I need to constantly train myself to be detached from what has happened.

The other more productive way to change is to accept that my natural state is a loving, peaceful, happy individual and live in this space. The first thought is: how am I going to do this? Then; this is ridiculous. But with perseverance like all new behaviours it gradually becomes easier. Now I am empowering myself, now I am working in the positive all the time, I really am working with my actualising tendency. I am growing hourly and daily. In my quiet times I can see the progress I am making. Now I can deal with the dysfunctional habits and behaviours that make effort to stop me reaching my goal of living as my natural self. As I am dealing with the defects in a positive rather than a negative manner I am now on a forward journey, growing with each step.

The key therefore is my thoughts. The more negative thoughts I have the more disillusioned and negative I become. Conversely the more positive my thoughts the more positive my outlook and actions. My experience is that when I feel low to check my thoughts. What sort of thoughts am I having? Are they thoughts of insecurity; I can't do that; they will never believe me; I'm not sure I should be doing this? Or are they thoughts that make me feel secure and powerful. I feel good today; I have done all I can to succeed in this mission; I am confident in my ability. One builds self esteem the other destroys it. My experience is that what I think is crucial to how I feel. The gross level of thought is easy to rectify but I realise there is a deeper more subtle level, an underpinning level that I need to conquer. Whatever caused the thought and subsequent behaviour is immaterial. I could have delved into my past, analysed my behaviour, looked at my parents and what happened in my childhood, looked at the emotionally crippling experiences I had had but basically this just gave me more data. At the end of the day I may be more enlightened as to what caused me to behave the way I did but it didn't help me to change. When I realised all I had to do was watch my thoughts and watch the subtle thoughts I created for myself I had something I could work with, something I was in control of. All I had to do was change those negative thoughts and views of the world and my self esteem would rise. After a while I began to notice that the more positive my thoughts the more light and peaceful I felt. The more positive thoughts I gave to myself the more positive I felt towards others. In Rogerian terms the more upr I gave to myself the more upr I felt for others. I do not wish to mislead you, this is not an easy path. My experience shows that I can't just manufacture positive thoughts but I am able to identify when I have thought myself into a difficult situation. I now understand that having the realisation that I am doing something that I want to change is more than half way towards changing that behaviour.

It's like being a gardener; first I have to look at the garden, identify what are weeds and what are flowers, remove the weeds and plant more flowers. But like every garden it doesn't finish there, a beautiful garden is the result of many years of tender loving care. I found this metaphor to be of great benefit especially when I had the realisation that in a garden flowers don't stand there looking at one another judging whether one has flowered to its potential or not. Or, whether another flower looks better than they do. They accept they are what they are. Therefore, as a flower my job is to accept who and what I am. As Ruth Sanford states (2001):

"Unconditional Positive Regard is a basic human need–pervasive and persistent".

To me Rogers' work is like the foundation on which to build a house. He has given us an insight into the foundation on which to build our life. Perhaps he was just reminding us of the rules to successful living that we had forgotten. Unconditional positive regard to all. As we pursue the attractiveness of conspicuous consumption and the need to 'fix' others we lose the ability to be unconditional. We appear to have settled for the second best option of being conditional. We have found it so easy to work with conditionality that it has become second nature. The result being that unconditionality appears so alien and difficult. We have learned to prefer the reward that analysis and intellectualisation bring rather than make the effort to focus on and find our true selves and build relationships based on unconditional love.

After revisiting Rogers' work after a number of years I am left with the feeling that he was either on the verge of a great discovery or knew something very special but didn't write about it. He has left us with the concepts of unconditional positive regard, empathy and congruence. He realised that if we hold these three tenets wonderful things can happen in our lives. He appears to be saying that if we live our lives according to the Person Centred Approach then we can really achieve something; we can get in touch with the real self, the fully functioning self, beyond materialism and behaviours.

I often wonder whether Rogers was actually making the effort to get us to get in touch with our spiritual self. The self that operates best when we show unconditional positive regard, the self that operates best with and through love. Is Rogers suggesting that through upr we are able to tune into our natural spiritual self? Was Rogers aware of the transformative power of what he is saying? That real success comes not by changing our behaviours from one stance to another but by acknowledging the very essence of our being.

Graham Harris lives in the Canary Islands where he pursues his current interests in photography, writing and spirituality.

REFERENCES

Bozarth, J. & Brodley, B. (1991). Actualisation: A functional concept. *Journal of Social Behaviour and Personality.*

Bozarth, J. (1993). Person centred therapy: A misunderstood paradigmatic difference. Paper To ADPCA. Maryville Tennessee.

Bozarth, J. (1998). Person centred therapy: A Revolutionary Paradigm. PCCS Books.

Bozarth, J. and Wilkins (2001). UPR. Unconditional positive regard. PCCS Books.

Heron, J. (1998). Sacred science: A revolutionary paradigm. PCCS Books.

Maslow, A. (1970). Motivation and personality. Harper & Row.

Mearns, D. (1994). Developing person centred counselling. Sage.

Mearns, D. & T. B. (1998). Person centred counselling in Action. Sage.

Rogers, C. (1954). Lecture to Oberlin College.

Rogers, C. (date unknown). The foundations of the person centred approach. Resident Fellow. Centre for Studies of the Person. La Jolla, California

Rogers, C. (1961). On becoming a person. Constable.

Rogers, C. (1973). My philosophy of interpersonal relations and how it grew. *J. Humanistic Psychology 13 (2),* 1973.

Rogers, C. (1980). A way of being. Houghton Mifflin.

Sandford, R. (2001). Unconditional positive regard: A misunderstood way of being. In Bozarth, and Wilkins (Ed). UPR unconditional positive regard. PCCS Books.

Wood, K.(1994). From the person centred approach to client centred therapy: What do some sixty years of experience suggest? Paper presented at the 3rd International Conference on Client Centred and Experiential Psychotherapy, Gmunden, Austria.

Who Am I? and Who Are All These Other People?

By Mhairi MacMillan

Twenty-seven years ago I first took part in a group designed, from person-centered principles, to offer 'experience and theory in facilitating groups' (FDI brochure, 1976). This chapter is an account of progress through many experiences in groups in the years following, groups which have ranged in size from twenty or so participants, through median groups of fifty or sixty to large groups of two hundred and fifty to three hundred. The group context has been that of residential workshop, international forum, cross-cultural communication workshop and specially convened meeting. My experiences in these groups is compared with my experiencing as a student in a 'school of esoteric education' which both overlaps and goes beyond these person-centered groups. Gradually it has become clear that the questions: Who am I? and Who are all these other people? are not only psychological and sociological questions, but also a spiritual enquiry.

'What I am is good enough if I can just be it'.

That first group was the FDI (Facilitator Development Institute) residential summer workshop held, that year, at the University of York, England. Charles (Chuck) Devonshire and colleagues Elke Lambers, Dave Mearns and Brian Thorne had recently brought these workshops to Britain.

I drove to York in a mixture of anticipation and fear. I had just met Mearns and Lambers who led a training course at a college of education, which I attended as a Guidance teacher in a Scottish High School. The taste afforded me on that course of the way of working called 'person-centered' and of the work of Carl Rogers enticed me to go to the FDI workshop the very next month.

I had never before had such a sense of freedom as I experienced at the York workshop. Talk about the expansion of the self-concept! Certainly, I was hungry for the social closeness available, and found the mix of nationalities, ages and personalities exhilarating. More importantly, I had the experience of being accepted for myself, of being listened to, of being a listener myself, and of not being responsible for a single other person. I was experiencing the person-centered approach in action.

I participated in the FDI workshop for three successive years. Carl Rogers, on his first visit to Britain in 1978 attended part of the third workshop. I remember first seeing him at the breakfast counter, deciding between one egg or two. I regret now to say that during the entire workshop I did not approach him or even address a single remark directly to him. This may be attributed to shyness or, more perversely, to my extreme difficulty in coping with the presence of anyone who might be considered 'famous'. The positive side of this is that I was not inclined to hero-worship and actually fell asleep in the back row at a special demonstration session with Rogers. I also felt that his coming (and going) as an interruption in my main business at the workshop which was, in short, me and my relationships with other people.

An incident I remember was when a Swiss woman wanted to audiotape the session with Rogers. Quite a fuss was made about asking permission of the group and somehow the woman was not allowed to tape. It turned out that this had been the main reason for her coming to the workshop, and soon afterwards, she left. What now seems significant to me is that I hardly noticed this and cared very little about this woman. I probably thought she was making far too much of a fuss. What's more, I did not know if anyone else cared about her, either.

Looking back at this time, it seems to me that it was primarily concerned with my developing *congruence*. And the quotation from Rogers that sums this up is: 'What I am is good enough if I can just be it' (which was given to me on a card at the Forum in La Jolla in 1987.) Of course, I was helped very much in this development by the acceptance of others, leading to greater self-acceptance, but the first step is in being what one is, at that moment. This congruence development was further consolidated in the next workshop described.

Moving outwards: Large Groups

In 1981, a team of Swiss adherents of the person-centered approach, including veterans of the La Jolla program, calling themselves 'the Swiss Group', convened a ten-day workshop in Zinal, an Alpine resort. This workshop broke new ground by eschewing 'staff/participant distinctions'. The Swiss Group wrote: 'Here, all are invited as equal participants. All may contribute, all may facilitate. There will be no designated staff, no "superstars"'. At the start, many participants still imagined the conveners would act as facilitators, and they had consistently to make it clear that they were not. Some people attributed the chaotic and frustrating beginning of the workshop to be due to the *lack* of facilitators. As time went on, the issue was forgotten, no longer of importance because virtually everyone was involved. There were certainly a number of people known to have 'facilitative skills' but my impression was that, for them, it was a definite relief and a great sense of freedom not to be in the role of facilitator.

Neither did the workshop have official translators. The conveners had simply stated: 'The workshop will take place in English, French and German. We hope you can speak at least one of these three languages'. Various developments followed. People wanted to speak their own national tongue and to hear those of others. A wide range of languages was heard. Translations became the responsibility of the whole group. At first, a few able linguists carried the load; then more and more people started to use languages they barely knew and even to translate for others who knew even less of a particular language than they did. Had there been 'official' translators, it is likely that participants would have refrained from trying out their own latent language skills and put the responsibility on to the translators. This is what happened in workshops, such as the Cross-cultural Communication workshops, where official translation was set up. It is a fine illustration of John Wood's point that conveners are best not to do for the group what it can do for itself (Wood, 1999, p. 142).

Those invited to Zinal were from a wide age range as well as many nationalities. They were encouraged to bring their families. At first, children and young people had their own groups and activities and some participants as well as parents helped and supervised them. Gradually, however, they came more and more into the main group, taking part in the same ways as the adults. One participant remarked that if the workshop had gone on longer (it lasted ten days) the hotel staff would have been drawn in as well. This illustrates one of the special features of this workshop: its inclusiveness (rather than exclusiveness). To emphasize the point: in this workshop, the coming together of the group and the sense of unity and connectedness among the participants seems to have been facilitated by the lack of designated facilitators and translators, which led people to look for resources within themselves, not from others.

This was a prime time for large groups. The La Jolla program was already running in the USA, and in Austria. There were others, principally in the USA and Brazil with which I am not familiar. In the same year as Zinal, the first Person-centered Approach to Cross-cultural Communications Workshop (to give the full title) took place, and these workshops continued for over ten years. The first International Forum on the Person-centered Approach–which has a large group component—was a year later, in 1982. The Forums continue, although shorter in duration than at first.

What is most personal is most general—development of empathy

I was asked to take the role of 'apprentice facilitator' for the 1980 FDI workshop. This was an important year for me: I was quitting my teaching job to move home and family hundreds of miles in order to take a post-graduate diploma in counseling. The workshop pattern had already been set whereby the facilitating team were put up as small group leaders and participants chose their small group largely on that basis. A large number of people disappeared into a group with one staff member and hardly ever emerged after that. Another large group formed around a second staff member. I was the new facilitator and the only woman on the staff and the smallest group came with me.

Having a staff role meant that I was less focused on myself and my own concerns, and more attuned to what the experience might be like for others—the beginning and essence of empathic relating. Of course, I probably would not have been invited on the staff had I not already shown some empathic sensibility. Neither is it a question of developing a more congruent way of relating followed by empathic understanding, for they grow together. Nevertheless, at this period in my life, empathy development took some precedence.

Istanbul 1988 (La Jolla Program International)

Another one off workshop was convened in 1988 in Istanbul, Turkey. Associates of the La Jolla program in California collaborated with Turkish alumni of the program to organize the workshop. I found that I was strongly drawn to go to Turkey, which I had not previously visited and immediately signed up when the schedule came out. I arrived in Istanbul after travelling all night and the same day one of the conveners phoned and asked if I would act as a small group leader. The response to the workshop from Turkish people had been greater than they had anticipated. I was thrilled to accept. The large group was composed of about 140 people, of whom over 100 were Turkish. There were a few participants from India, the rest European or American. This was my first experience of a workshop taking place within a culture different from the western European-north American one. I was profoundly affected to hear the *ezan* (call to prayer) early in the morning and throughout the day, and to see all around a skyline punctuated by minarets.

The La Jolla program is run as small group meeting with the large group convened at the beginning, at the end and half-way through, at which time the small groups change composition. There is little struggle about when and how to break into small groups and the make-up of at least the first set of groups is pre-decided. Having only experienced the FDI and Cross-cultural workshop 'models', I had come to perceive them as the norm and the La Jolla program (which in fact had begun before the others) as rather *un*-natural. My experience and that of some other European participants perhaps influenced the format a little, with (I believe) a small amount of additional time given to the large group. At the mid-way changeover of small groups, most of the group I was with chose to stay together. A few people left and a few others joined.

Language became an issue both in the large group and in my own 'small' group (of twenty-five people). The official workshop language was English—often an international 'lingua franca'—but at least one Turkish participant objected strongly to her mother tongue's disenfranchisement. Some of us supported her, but her speaking Turkish was criticized by a German participant for he, too, had to speak a foreign language, and he could not understand Turkish. The question of language brings out many issues around identity, acceptance of the other, power, how a majority (in number) is made into a minority by language dominance, which has been called 'English language imperialism'.

At the end of this workshop I experienced what can only be described as a deep grieving. During the workshop, I had been invited to the home of a Turkish participant and was again invited to stay with her when it ended. I spent the first afternoon in tears feeling complete deprivation; then we went out into the city and drank ayran and I began to feel better. I had by then taken part in groups for twelve years and this was the first time I had experienced such an intense reaction at the end. It wasn't because of the delights of the workshop location. It had taken place in a college in Bebek and those of us who were residential (less than a third of participants) had endured bunk-bedded accommodation, cold showers and a fair number of mosquito bites until we learned to keep the windows shut despite the heat.

So, why did I feel this sense of utter deprivation, as if I had been torn from my closest family, my most close companions? I cannot answer this definitively, yet I believe it has something to do with the sense of *loss* of the very oneness or wholeness that I experienced on the workshop.

<u>Reaching the parts individual therapy cannot reach?</u>

At the 1995 International Forum on the Person-centered Approach in Greece, Colin Lago and I made a presentation entitled 'Large Groups–Dodging the Issue?'. Lago (1994) had suggested that 'our cultural beliefs in individualism, intensified in recent decades by political and economic forces, have had alienating effects upon our society....Group work in general and large groups in particular, offer a forum in which these complex issues of relatedness, the management of power, decision making and active democracy can be explored by participants'. But what if these large groups continue, in their concentration on individual feelings especially past emotional trauma, to perpetuate that same cult of the individual? One way that this is fostered is by the continuation of the 'counseling' type of response that is learned in training school, and modeled, consciously or unconsciously both by trainees and by long-time practicing counselors and therapists. May this not obscure for us the growth and development of the experiencing of the group itself?

In the summer of 1996, three Large Group seminars were offered in different parts of Britain. The invitation was to people who would like to discuss their experience in large groups and to try to make some sense of it. This venture was supported by the British Academy which enabled John K Wood and Lucila Machado Assumpcao to come from Brazil, joining Colin Lago and myself as conveners of the seminars. Participants' experiences ranged from 'community meetings' on training courses to the groups of 2-300 already mentioned. A wide range of ideas and concerns were discussed (Lago and MacMillan, 1999, p. 36-39) and were collated under the following headings:

Technical aspects of large groups, convening, context and setting
Research methodologies for large groups
An understanding of meaning (of, and in, large groups)
Exploration of emotional life–'expectations' and 'fears'
The challenge of creating the core conditions

John Wood's reflections on the seminars are summed up in three ways.

1. Is it possible to think together about our collective behavior as well as focus attention on the subjective feelings of individuals in the group?
2. What about the Hawthorne effect? As applied to large groups, it implies change may be brought about in the group (and individuals) by the very activity of meeting as a group and attending to the process intentionally.
3. Each seminar participant seemed to bring a different aspect of group experience into the discussion. Each person is putting into words an expression of part of the phenomenon of large groups...the phenomenon is actually speaking for itself, through itself, that is, through its parts.

A number of people expressed the wish for further large group meetings, but no definite plans were made to organize one.

However, following these seminars, a large group *was* convened by Peggy Natiello and her associates in Sedona, Arizona in January 1998 (Lago and MacMillan, 1999, 39-41; Natiello, 2001, ch 11). This immediately posed a dilemma for me. I had enrolled on a retreat course at the Beshara School of

Intensive Esoteric Education for six months. However, I talked with the principal of the school who agreed to 'consult' in the tradition of the school. I do not know exactly what this entails. But the result of the consultation was that 'it seemed good that I should prepare to attend the large group.' Accordingly I made the necessary preparations before I started on the course. As the time drew near, my supervisors on the course were doubtful about the necessity of my being away; the principal, however, simply said, 'She has to go; although we may never know why'. Accordingly I left the school (temporarily) and traveled to Arizona.

It seems to me now that the greatest significance of the Sedona workshop was that it took place at all. Sixty people from all over the United States and Europe gathered together in a remote place in the Arizona desert. If it were the case that I had 'had to go', it was in a sense also true that everyone else 'had' to be there. This is not making a claim for the 'specialness' of this event; what was special was the deliberate conscious choice of everyone to participate.

Yet I must confess to some disappointment with the outcome. I believe that the 'conscious intention' to take part was somehow squandered, leaving me with the question: what is the basis on which a sense of mutuality can be established? I found myself almost unmoved by personal stories of trauma, of devastating child-hood or the deaths of close relatives. It may have been because I had heard some of the stories before, from the same people. I think this is a key: had these people been clients in a counseling situation, I would have accepted the necessity of telling the story over and over again. This was not a therapy situation but I seemed to find myself being put into the role of a therapist and having to be empathic and apparently unconditionally accepting. There were many therapists present and sound, sincere therapeutic responses were made. I felt very distant and unable to say so. Perhaps my 'therapist' persona was too strong to be easily overruled.

At Sedona, there was a sense of communion with the natural surroundings, with the world, one third of the way around the globe from my home and with the former inhabitants of that place. But this was not enough to lift us above the competing demands of going to visit tourist sights (on the one hand) and focusing on 'expressing feelings' on the other.

Tasting the Unity

"I share with many others the belief that the truth is unitary, even though we will never be able to know this unity" (Rogers, 1959, p. 190). In some large groups, however, at a particular stage of the development of the group, there emerge certain phenomena that point toward, or give a taste of, unity. Coulson has put it thus:

For many of us the sense of union or community with other group members is one of the most deeply satisfying outcomes of participation in these workshops. Sometimes this feeling expands beyond the group to encompass a sense of connectedness with all humankind, or even with the whole universe. It seems that experience in a workshop may more clearly illuminate one's individual identity and at the same time one may be taken up into a new whole that is somehow larger than the self on its own. (Coulson, 1999)

Another group participant reported a similar experience with regard to different languages used in the group—or, rather, the superseding of language difference, when he found himself—a native English speaker and rather a reticent one—actually speaking in French during a community meeting (MacMillan and Lago, 1995). Others have reported understanding the meaning of what has been said, in a language, not known to them, when in the later stages of a group workshop.

Such reports are examples of a different kind of consciousness operating for these people. Coulson again:

When I have experienced this condition, my self-consciousness, my internal monologue, even my thoughts and my sense of time all seem to be temporarily suspended. My self-created barriers are lowered...(Coulson, 1999, p. 171)

This is associated with an absorption in the present moment of the process, a loss of conscious self-interest, with the source of any utterance seeming to be from somewhere deeper within the organism. This being present in the moment has the effect of also being facilitative for other group members. In a study of 'Participants' experiences of facilitative moments' in large groups, 'being facilitative' was connected by some with 'the time of greatest engagement in the group' (MacMillan and Lago, 1995, p. 603).

It is agreed that the group has to reach a certain 'stage' or 'state' before these phenomena are experienced. It has even been described by some as an 'altered state of consciousness' (MacMillan and Lago, 1995). There is some evidence as to what helps this state to be reached, and, perhaps more significant, what hinders its development.

The sense of connection, of shared human experiencing is neither mysterious nor dramatic. As Rogers put it, 'What is most personal is most general' (Rogers, 1961, p. 26). It does not only happen in person-centered groups. In a psychodrama group, Natiello found that 'what attracted me most about the experience was a sense of connection that grew between the 23 of us as a result of sharing in one another's lives, stories and struggles' (Natiello, 2001, p. 122). A sense of connection is seen, therefore, to build up inevitably unless it should be hindered or even shattered by antagonistic factors, some of which will be examined later.

But a taste of unity goes beyond a sense of connectedness with others, profound though that may be. John K Wood, who writes most thoughtfully on large groups, puts it thus, 'In large groups, the properties of the whole come through the individual' and paraphrases the philosopher Martin Heidegger, 'The part [individual] is a place for "presencing" the whole' (Wood, 1999, p. 148).

There are some obvious dangers here for the person who is not grounded sufficiently in her/his own sense of reality. They may either feel obliterated within the group like an ant or a bee is within the colony, or assume grandiose or megalomaniac personality characteristics, believing they can 'read' a group entirely through their own feelings. Wood sounds a monitory note:

> "This extremely important potential of the group should perhaps be accompanied by a warning announcement. Perceiving the unity without participants—at the same time—maintaining an adequate awareness of their personal reality, can result in 'epidemic' emotions.
>
> "...*Emphasizing* the group as a whole, *without* attention to the constructive experience of individual members and without an ambience which includes empathy and acceptance may not only be unhelpful, but even harmful to participants (Wood, 1999, 149, emphasis in the original)

What is called for is the perception of the 'multiplicity in unity', holding the tension between oneself as a unique individual (albeit dyed by the coloring of time and culture) and as this 'place' in which the whole may take its form. It is vital, also, to remember that the whole is ultimately larger than the group itself, and the group, indeed, is in turn a place for the presencing of *that* whole. This resonates with 'the belief that the truth is unitary, even though we may never be able to know the unity' (Rogers, 1959, p. 190).

Helping' factors

It is not possible to prescribe factors or conditions that inevitably lead to the sense of multiplicity within the unity of the group—and by extension, within the unity of, say, the universe. It is necessary to point out that the whole is not a 'thing', but an 'unfolding' or movement, or, as Wood (1999, p. 148) reminds us, an 'active absence'. Some writers, however, have pointed to a number of factors, which they perceive as helpful, if not indispensable, for a sense of connectedness. These resonate with my own experience in groups.

Undertaking the organization of a large group is not a light task. Consideration of location, timing, duration, financial risk as well as the potential participants and how they will be informed or selected, are all involved. Consensus should be reached on the purpose of the meeting, the role of the conveners once the meeting starts and arrangements (or not) for technological support such as microphones or translators.

As John Wood put it:

In every stage of the development of the workshop, the organizers are agents of the group. Their job is to do what the group *cannot* do for itself. When the participants are finally face to face, organizers are no longer needed, as the group can direct itself. (Wood, 1999, 159, emphasis in the original.)

Therefore, a deep 'conscious intention' is needed, not only on the part of the conveners, but also from the participants. People come to a group looking for a holiday in a nice place, to meet old friends or lovers and to make new ones, to practice what they have learned in counseling school, and so on. All of these have probably been part of my motivation at some time or other. But there needs also to be a willingness to welcome whatever happens and to allow personal interest to become subservient to the emerging whole.

MacMillan and Lago's (1995) research on what is facilitative in large groups drew responses indicating the importance of 'being present' whether official facilitator or participant, and how significant it is to continue to hear and attend to each unique individual.

At the most basic, a look, a touch or even another's attentive silence were experienced as facilitative and it was confirmed that being directly responded to can prove a powerful experience (MacMillan and Lago, 1995, p. 605).

'Hindering' factors

It cannot be overlooked that many large groups do not attain the stage of sensing the wholeness. Many things can get in the way of this and I outline some of them here.

The effect of counseling and counseling training

Since the time of large groups, there has been, in Britain at least, a huge mushrooming of counseling and psychotherapy training courses. The original British directors of FDI all moved from convening the workshops into counselor training, first independently then within universities. They carried with them, however, the incorporation of a group experience–known as the 'community group' into their programs. These groups had around thirty members, the number of trainees on the course, so fell far short of the one to three hundred participants in some of the large groups mentioned above. Those who took part in them, however, believe that they had taken part in a *large* group. Because these were training groups, there was an expectation on the participants to 'use' the group to work out personal issues (no such expectation existed in other groups) and an element of assessment, whether by tutors, peers or self. Many of them found the so-called 'large' group a difficult, even frightening experience. On the other hand, others found that they could operate in the group in apparent accordance with 'person-centered' principles, not necessarily in an inauthentic way, but with the danger of the assumption building up that this was how it should be done.

Complacency

This can lead directly to another hindrance, 'Falsely assuming that previous successful experience automatically applies in a new situation' (Wood, 1999, p.152). Whether one is a 'designated' facilitator or a previous participant in groups, it is very tempting to follow a familiar formula, instead of which it must be recognized that every group is a new situation, and while earlier learning may help, it cannot simply be applied again. The 'self that one truly is' is not fixed, but is ever revealing itself in reactions, feelings and thoughts about what is *currently* happening. So, for example, there is a subtle difference between a person hearing and responding from the heart to another, however unrehearsed and awkward, and one in trained counselor mode practicing empathic responding, however fluent and polished.

Tyranny of feelings

Expression of personal feeling is an important currency in the group. Without it the group would be arid, barren, no better than an academic discussion. But the group can get stuck in a pattern of feeling expression and response to this. The feelings may center on personal pain and difficulty or on as apparently trivial matters as how the chairs are organized in the circle. One participant in a Cross-cultural Communication workshop who had taken this title at face value was continually frustrated that no one responded to her desire to examine political issues such as gender and sexuality within the group. "'Why do feelings come before these things", she asked. "It seems there is a tyranny of feelings here'" (McIlduff and Coghlan, 1989, p. 81). My experience in the Sedona workshop bears this out.

Group incongruence

Inauthenticity may produce its worst effects when it arises within a staff group. 'Group incongruence or deceit' is probably the most serious 'limiting factor' on the development of 'experiential communality' (Bebout 1974). I have been a staff member when such a situation arose. The FDI workshop in Norfolk, England in 1993 was the most difficult, unproductive, and even destructive that I have experienced. There had been a decision, apparently consensual, made by the staff that this workshop would have a training emphasis; that is, that the group would be invited explicitly to look at its own process during the course of the workshop. Later, when stresses appeared both in the total group and in the staff, it emerged that two of the staff had not been genuinely convinced of this aspect, but had 'gone along with it'. Moreover, some if not all of the staff had personal issues that were not carefully dealt with. Trust amongst the staff members was minimal and, again, this remained an unspoken difficulty.

I became further and further removed from my own 'organismic valuing', (an operational definition of congruence in groups) and was unable to discuss this even in staff meetings. At one point I became furiously angry with a participant whom I felt had expectations of me that did not fit at all who I really was. In the end, I did return to a state of congruence—after a sleepless night, all superfluous feelings fell away and only the core sentiment remained—and was able, in the last session, to speak authentically in the group.

This might well have been a difficult workshop in any case, but the splits and incongruences within the staff group contributed to the end result of fragmentation in the group, without even a whiff of a sense of unity. It is noteworthy that even in this disastrous situation, some individuals still felt benefit from the workshop (Barkham, 1999).

Lack of a 'shared reality'

Maureen O'Hara has described another group process that ended in fragmentation. Again, unresolved tensions and 'some conceptual disagreements which we had somehow minimized in our enthusiasm to create the program' ended with 'our community had broken down.....we did not have a shared frame of reference...we were in two completely different consciousness states, and our leaders were in conflict' (O'Hara, 1995, pp. 137-138).

Some understanding of this event led O'Hara to realize:

> If the full expression of feelings is to be contained within a group, people need to establish a shared reality, a shared context, a shared commitment to mutual benefit.... Authentic expression of diverse

positions easily drives people apart when not everyone commits to empathic understanding and mutual respect (O'Hara, 1995, p. 138)

At first thought, it might seem that the person-centered approach might in itself be enough to ensure the shared reality and context that O'Hara mentions. There are many reasons why this may not work out. For a start, it is merely an approach, 'a way of being from which one confronts a situation' (Wood, 1995, p. 163). As such it can engender a commitment to certain values which can be shared in a group of people, but if these shared values become an ideology or dogma, creativity is badly impaired. I have come to dread the accusation heard in-groups: 'That's not person-centered!'

Another application of the approach is to client-centered therapy, but, as Wood points out, 'the psychology of client-centered therapy does not adequately explain applications of the person-centered approach'. It seems, though, that that is what can happen in groups when, as described above, 'counseling mode' takes over. When the person-centered approach operates in large groups, it has to expand to match that context, and can only provide containment depending on the concept of the *person* (the human being) and of the wider standing in which humans exist, which is prevalent among the group participants.

'A shared reality': education at the Beshara school

My concept of the person has been refined through studying at the Beshara school of esoteric education (see www.beshara.org). The overarching posture (approach) at Beshara is from the point of view of the Unity of Being, explicitly stating that which is implied in Rogers's (1959) remark that 'the truth is unitary'. It can be stated as 'Being is one, though variously named' (E Wood, 1974), and amplified in the following statement:

> ......what is offered through its [Beshara's] education is precisely this all-inclusive point of view which is at once esoteric and exoteric, beautiful and intensely practical, and which by its very nature demands a choice of us all as human beings. The choice is whether to accept to live our lives as **our** lives, under the illusion of separation; or to accept the Truth, albeit only as an idea, that our lives are not **our** lives but are extensions of Universal Life in a relative form as us (Young, 2000).

From the courses at Beshara, I learned more about the meaning of what is called Unconditional Positive Regard. I experienced being totally accepted, and perceived the total acceptance of every person (and anything else) as a manifestation of the One. Of course, at the human level, judgements are continually occurring. I saw more clearly that I am continually making judgements of others and of myself, which condition the positivity of the regard I hold for 'us'. It is not possible to rid oneself completely of judgements, but they can be seen for what they are–conditioned and conditional–and let go or suspended and invested with no importance.

Consider Rogers's description of unconditionality:

> If the self-experiences of another are perceived by me in such a way that no self-experience can be discriminated as more or less worthy of positive regard than any other…(Rogers, 1959, p. 209)

(and similarly for unconditional *self*-regard). This is essentially the same as concepts in spiritual traditions such as 'equanimity' or 'emotional balance' (Wood, 1974, pp. 73-80). Theses notions acknowledge that there are things we like and dislike but we need not (and should not) let likes and dislikes affect our actions.

In my experience it is easier for me to suspend my judgements in a counseling situation than in a group, or in everyday living. Being on the Beshara courses helped me to become aware and mindful of my judging habits (see also MacMillan, 1999). Purton, too, has said that 'the concept of unconditional positive regard cannot properly be employed without taking a view of the person that is essentially spiritual' (Purton, 1998, p. 24).

The key points confirmed at Beshara (in relation to this paper) are, thus, the Oneness of Being and the Uniqueness of each form of the multiplicity within it, and consequently the illusive nature of a separate autonomous self. These assertions are common to the major spiritual traditions (many sources, examples: Epstein 1995, Halevi 1985, Hirtenstein 1999, Kraft 1984, Sells 1994, Underhill 1984, Wood 1974). From this (universal) point of view, the answer to the questions, Who am I? And who are all these other people? is that we are all aspects or facets of that One Being. We can paraphrase 'To be that self which one truly is' as: 'To be that self which one is, in Truth'; here meaning that all-inclusive Truth, sometimes known as God.

My learning from experience in large groups involves meaning at both the personal and the collective-intuitive levels. The meaning of 'myself' to me is both that I found an autonomous less-conditioned (if not unconditioned) entity, not fixed but continually unfolding, and that this entity can somehow be relinquished into the whole flowing through the group and the individuals in it. Real acceptance of oneself and of others' right to exist as *themselves*, in Truth, is more urgently needed now than ever and anything, such as a person-centered approach, which can point towards such reconciliation, not as a dogma or ideology, should be fostered.

Mhairi MacMillan has over twenty years' experience in person-centered group work, in Britain, Europe and worldwide. She has headed a university counseling service, lectured in counseling and authored a number of book chapters. Currently she works independently as a counselor, supervisor and small group facilitator. Alternatively, she studies at the Beshara School and tries to improve her painting.

REFERENCES

Barkham, J. (1999). The facilitator development institute (Britain) workshops. In C. Lago & M. MacMillan (Eds.), *Experiences in relatedness: Groupwork and the person-centred approach*. Ross-on-Wye: PCCS Books.

Bebout, J. (1974). It takes one to know one: Existential-Rogerian concepts in encounter groups. In D. Wexler & L. Rice (Eds.), *innovations in client-centered therapy*. New York: Wiley.

Coulson, A. (1999). Experiences of separateness and unity in person-centred groups. In C. Lago & M. MacMillan (Eds.), *Experiences in relatedness*. Ross-on-Wye: PCCS Books.

Epstein, M. (1995). *Thoughts without a thinker*. London: Duckworth.

FDI (1976) Facilitator Development Institute Residential Summer workshop brochure.

Halevi, Z. (1985). *Adam and the Kabbalistic tree*. London: Gateway Books.

Hirtenstein, S. (1999). *The unlimited mercifier: The spiritual life and thought of Ibn 'Arabi*. Oxford, Anqa and Ashland, Oregon: White Cloud Press.

Kraft, K. (1984). *Zen: tradition and transition*. London: Rider.

Lago, C. (1994). Therapy for a masturbatory society: The need for connectedness and community; *Counselling*, 5(2), 120-124.

Lago, C. & MacMillan, M. (Eds.). (1999). *Experiences in relatedness: Groupwork and the person-centred approach*. Ross-on-Wye: PCCS Books.

MacMillan, M. & Lago, C. (1995). The facilitation of large groups. In R. Hutterer, G. Pawlowsky, P. Schmid & R. Stipsits (Eds.), *Client-centered and Experiential Psychotherapy: A paradigm in motion*. Frankfurt: Peter Lang.

MacMillan, M. (1999). In you there is a universe: Person-centred counselling as manifestation of the breath of the merciful. In Irene Fairhurst (Ed.), *Women writing in the person-centred approach*. Ross-on-Wye: PCCS Books.

McIlduff, E. & Coghlan, D. (1989). Process facilitation in a cross-cultural communication workshop, *Person-centered Review*, 4(1), 77-98.

Natiello, P. (2001). *The Person-centred approach: A passionate presence*. Ross-on-Wye: PCCS Books.

O'Hara, M. (1995). Streams: On becoming a postmodern person. In M. Suhd (Ed.), *Positive regard: Carl Rogers and other notables he influenced*. Palo Alto: Science and Behavior Books.

Purton, C. (1998). Unconditional positive regard and its spiritual implications. In B. Thorne & E. Lambers (Eds.), *Person-centred therapy: a European perspective*. London: Sage.

Rogers, C. R. (1959). A theory of therapy, personality and interpersonal relations. In S. Koch (Ed.), *Psychology: A study of a science*, Vol 3; New York: McGraw-Hill.

Sells, M. (1994). *Mystical languages of unsaying*. Chicago: University of Chicago Press

Underhill, E (1984). *The spiritual life*. Oxford: Mobray.

Wood, E. (1974). *The glorious presence*. Wheaton, Illinois: Theosophical Publishing.

Wood, J. K. (1995). The Person-centered approach: Toward an understanding of its implications. In R. Hutterer, G. Pawlowsky, P. Schmid & R. Stipsits (Eds.), *client-centered and experiential psychotherapy: a paradigm in motion*. Frankfurt: Peter Lang.

Wood, J. K. (1999). Towards an understanding of large group dialogue and its implications. In C. Lago & M. MacMillan (Eds.). *Experiences in Relatedness: groupwork and the person-centred approach*. Ross-on-Wye:: PCCS Books.

Young, P. (2000). United by oneness: global considerations for the present; transcript of a talk on the Beshara website, www.beshara.org.

First Hundred Years Are the Hardest

C. H. Patterson

Rogers was born 100 years ago. But client-centered therapy may be dated from 1940, when Rogers presented it in a paper at the University of Minnesota. It was reported that it did not get an enthusiastic reception. Minnesota's reception was cool for many years. I went to Minnesota in 1947 to a position as Personal Counselor in the Veterans Administration following a period of study with Rogers at the University of Chicago. My visit to the Director of the University Counseling Center was cool. E. H. Porter, a former student and then colleague of Rogers, accompanied me to Minnesota to be interviewed for the position of Director of the Counseling Center. He declined the position when he learned that he would not be allowed to focus the Center on the client-centered approach. In the fall of 1947 I enrolled in the doctoral program in counseling with Gilbert Wrenn. From a source I consider reliable I was told—after I received my diploma in 1955—that the former Director of the Counseling Center had said that if he had anything to do with it I would not receive a degree from the University. Ironically, it was he, who was then Dean of the Graduate School, who handed me my diploma. It was only later that I learned the partial source of this attitude. Minnesota had wanted the program for counselor education that was given to Rogers at the University of Chicago.

Minnesota was no doubt not the only University that responded coolly to the client-centered approach to psychotherapy. The so-called Minnesota approach (Patterson, 1966) was widely accepted. But over a period of some 20 years, client-centered counseling became widely accepted in counselor education programs during the 60s and 70s.

But the tide has turned again. Client-centered therapy is alive, but not well—that is not in the United States. It is doing well in many other places—the UK, Europe, South America.

We are living in the age of technology, and the field of counseling and psychotherapy, indeed the field of human relations in general, is becoming technologized. The practice of psychotherapy is thus a matter of intervening in the therapist-client relationship with certain techniques or skills, operating on the client to achieve certain outcomes chosen—or considered desirable by—the counselor or therapist. Counselors or therapists are now expert technicians with a kit of tools—or skills.

There is a paradox in the current trends in psychotherapy and medicine: while medicine is moving away from more invasive procedures to less invasive procedures in treatment, particularly in surgery, psychotherapy is moving toward more invasive procedures. For every intervention there is a risk—every form of surgery has failures. There are also risks in psychological interventions.

So the near future of client centered therapy is dim; it will persist in other countries, but I am convinced that because it is so basically true, and right, that eventually, in 20 or 30 years, the field of psychotherapy will come around to it.

REFERENCE

Patterson, C. H. (1966). The Minnesota point of view. Chapter 1 in *Theories of counseling and psychotherapy*. New York: Harper.

Relationaldynamics: A Greek Reading Of The Person-Centered Learning and Education

Grigoris Mouladoudis
Alexandros Kosmopoulos

This chapter deals with the *Relationaldynamics* education of the person, as a Greek person-centered approach to learning and education. We present the principles and the primary concepts of *Relationaldynamics*, as well as the particular goals for the becoming of the student in a *person*. Finally, we discuss the three phases and the stages of the *Relationaldynamics* learning model.
Keywords: *Relationaldynamics*, relationship, person, person-centered education, readiness, dialogue.

"The pathway of reality is paved by utopias...we don't expect the world to change in order to function."

In whatever is characterized and further analyzed by educators or politicians up to date as the cause of misfortune in the schools' general effectiveness, we would discern as a prime-cause the lack of coherence, connection and relation between the student and her work. In older times it used to be valid to hold students and teachers by the ethics of adaptation (conformity), within schoolwork; to her surprise today one could observe that schools insist on functioning by the above. The participation of teachers is low; they appear to be afraid, tightened and nervous. The students are also tied up with the school through the obligation of an institutional frame. But let's think for one moment: when the conventional collapses, what is it that will "keep children in school"? (e.g. the parent's motto until recently: "My child, learn to read and write to be successful in life", nowadays that the financial success of a school graduate not only does not depend directly on the years of studies but, many times is an occasion of inverse ratio).

Specifically in modern age, so rich in seductive temptations, where the efforts for learning are not appreciated. So, does the parents' motto have any value today? And the question remains: what is it that can connect the students with the school today? Their love for learning? This school is dead. The students know that the school isn't important for her, because it does not deal with fundamental as interesting subjects of life and does not live in relation with the things. If it wasn't for the need to obtain a certificate, they would abandon. The great problem and at the same time the significant factors of each reform in education is the existence:

a. **Qualitative criteria.** Mainly because the school for children and adolescents needs to be a place that educates and will respond to their interests.
b. **Participation of students and teachers in the learning process.** This intellectual and sentimental participation is low.

These two significant factors in education are in the opposite direction. The technocratic changes do not save the school because they are not changes that touch upon the substance. Therefore what elements would be positive for the school apart from the creation of personal motives, which will internally connect the school with the students' interests and needs? What else, that is to say, but the abolition of the *un-relational* (without relationship), which reign over school and its replacement by a functional and direct "relationship" between the student and her school education. This relationship alone gives meaning to the studies and incorporates them in the developmental process of a child or teenager.

Relationaldynamics of the Person: Principles and Primary Concepts

Relationaldynamics of the Person—in Greek *Shesiodynamici,* the word *shesis* means relationship—is an approach which regards the educational functioning and action as a product of the student's personal relationship with the teacher. It has as main researching and educational objects the study of the educative relationship as relationship of the human being with herself, with the learning "good" and with the other: of the teacher with the student, of the student with her peer and with the teacher. The mission of this educational orientation is based on the level of enhancement of the relationship—as an entity of central importance—to a genuine and person-centered one. *Relationaldynamics,* places great emphasis on the consideration of education not as a static but as a fluid and dynamic process. Its effectiveness is a product of the facilitative development by the teacher of the progressing relational and communicative dynamics multiplied by the "readiness" of the student (Kosmopoulos, 1990a, 1990b, 1994).

Relationaldynamics mainly influenced by the tenets of the humanistic, phenomenological psychology (Giorgi, 1995; Rogers, 1961, 1970, 1980; Spinelli, 1989; Wertz, 1992) and person-centered approach to education (DeCarvalho, 1991; Combs, 1988; Hill, 1994; Richards & Combs, 1992; Rogers, 1969, Rogers, 1983, Rogers & Freiberg, 1994). It also influenced by the notion and the psychospiritual being of the *person* as acquired in the ancient Greek philosophy and the Christian-Orthodox church (Mouladoudis & Patrikiou, 2002) as well as the personalistic philosophical thought, especially the philosophy of Martin Buber (1958, 1965a, 1965b). Specifically, *Relationaldynamics* is influenced and can be seen as a new fruitful synthesis (Mouladoudis, 2001, p. 10; Rose 2001, p. 2), between Martin Buber's philosophical thought and Carl Rogers' Person-Centered approach.

This is what *Relationaldynamics* do:

a. It is the educational proposal of relationship. It stresses the importance of the interhuman, interpersonal (and not facade) and educative relationship and its designation in a central factor of educative and therapeutic changes in the human being. Carl Rogers himself sees psychotherapy as a contact and genuine relationship between two or more individuals that heals with the dynamics that is practiced, for the sake of its qualitative characteristics.

b. Education is supported in the releasing force and in the developing dynamics of authentic (genuine) relationships between the teacher and the student. How genuine is the relationship, how pedagogic, and how efficient is it today? How these become and can become? For this reason it deepens and researches the educative relationship, as well as the practiced dynamics of genuineness.

c. It distinguishes the "communication" from the "relationship" and the "encounter". It considers as educative and therapeutic exploitable the "relationship" and seeks a relational communication. There take place verbal and non-verbal, visible and invisible messages. A communication that is inspired by the sense of a "common place" or a "bond" that connects the participants.

d. It spotlights and reveals in the field of Human Sciences the significance of "dynamics", a concept mainly of physics. Thus, is defended an education that from one point has direction, vision, beginnings, but from the other shapes the content, the methodology and its "rules" in dynamic interaction and relation with the human, natural, technical and social environment. As for its substance a robust, bold and fighting education is created, and at the same time flexible and adapted to the individual and to the conditions. Of course, in this frame, everything is placed under the responsible disposal and possibility of the interested party; the teacher keeps the essential, but "waived" role of the *facilitator* of the other in the successful conduct of the work that concerns the other personally (e.g. her learning or her growth).

e. It believes that the essential point in education that releases, develops and also forms beneficially and substantially the "person" is held secretively, internally, through the multifunctional relational context of the dynamics that is developed in the student. For this reason it gives priority in an education that nourishes the relationship with the genuine self, both for the student and the teacher. An education not of the behavior, but of the consciousness and freedom of the person.

f. The "heart" of *Relationaldynamics* attitude and behavior of the teacher is her dialogical ability. The "dialogue" is not only energy or a form of communicative process. It is most of all a philosophical and psychological attitude of the soul, the highest expression of *Relationaldynamics* quality of the participants in dialogue. Dialogical can be characterized the teacher that not only is proved a skillful operator of "dialogue's" art, but is placed herself—as a person—in the dynamic situation of a "dialogue" as co-researcher. This means that she does not rely on herself. The dialogical attitude testifies dialogical life, which is identical with the "life in adventure".

It is an expression and a process of psychosomatics movement initially to the depths of the self and, then, to other, the interlocutor or the fellowman. "Dialogue without movement of the souls is not comprehended, because the dialogue itself is simultaneously a psychological and intellectual, energy of the personality (exit from I and path to the Thou), multidimensional, unified and continuous. It is a movement towards persons, ideas and events. The objectives of this movement serve in time and place the change, (as the stability), and proportionally fix it as a movement to the other, or as a movement that constitutes "constancy mobile" and the opposite of the tranquility. As a final point the dialogic movement constitutes an existential type of a person for its truth because it constitutes operation of re-establishment of harmony, through the "unit of the contraries" (Buber, 1963, 13-17).

In the psychological and intellectual dimension of this movement, is not recognized the dynamic plenitude if it is not included in its significance and intention. The movement that is observed in the dialogue has deepest roots inside, in each participant's personality. These roots nourish and influence its dynamics, as the direction that it takes. Our personal culture as human beings and our indwelling constitute basic conditions of the dialogic movement.

Our personal "readiness" determines the quality and the effectiveness of a dialogue to a maximum degree. Readiness is a fruit both of our psychological sociability and maturity, as well as of our intellectual culture. For this reason it is always difficult to distinguish dialogue and love, as actions of a unified personality, because both are forms and products of psychomotor energy and depend immediately from the interpersonal achievements of the parties in dialogue. Love is the substance of "the life in dialogue". In this genuinely relational environment, the process to the knowledge mutates into a process to the strange, into "erotic view" and in *Koinonia* [communion] with the "good" (the Greek word *Koinonia* means an intimate communication or interchange, the act of sharing or holding in common, thoughts, emotions or feelings).

Relationaldynamics: Particular Goals for the Becoming of the Student in a Person

The concept of the *person* includes the characteristics that attributed to it by the phenomenology of Merleau Ponty (1976), and the French philosophical-psychological school of Mounier (1952) and journal *Esprit*. Specifically by psychotherapists, it includes the elements that have been reported, by Allport (1968), Caruso (1964) and Frankl (1985a). However, the concept of the person mostly includes the characteristics of "the highest fulfillment of self" as defined by Maslow (1987) and of the "fully-functioning person" as defined by Rogers (1961) and analysed or interpreted by Schmid (1998), Patterson and Hidore (1997). Person-Centered approach has a revolutionary—for the human relations—viewpoint at man's being as a "person" and gives to the concept a special meaning (Rogers & Schmid, 1998; Schmid, 1998b; Stewart, 2000, personal communication). The "person" in Rogers's thought represents the ideal of the human being's actualisation; either as the goal of life or of therapy, "is a *process*, not a state of being. It is a direction, not a destination" (Rogers, 1961, p. 186). Rogers does draw a difference between the self and the "person". For him the self is just one aspect of the "person". Rogers's view is that the self is defined as the way in which the individual consciously views himself or herself, that means the self is a perception by the "person". The whole "person", includes every part of the individual—the cognitive, the emotional, the physiological/organismic aspect—the totality of the individual" (Seeman, 2000, personal communication).

Relationaldynamics—from its part—underlining the phenomenological view of the person, which stresses that personal experience is the highest authority and that the study of the person is based on the method of studying individual ways of perceiving the world. It also distinguishes the terms *person, personality* and *individual*. The person cooperates with the personality and many times or usually its actions are manifested through the actions of the personality. Though, they represent two separate and not identified entities and concepts. The person constitutes the stamp of originality and the source of the utmost inner freedom. It is both psychological—complementary but does not coincide with the personality—and spiritual entity. When the person is distinguished and when it rules over the personality, then the personality is in a position to ignore even its individualistic "self-interest" frame.

The particular goals of *Relationaldynamics* for the becoming of the student in a person are:

a. The uniqueness of the Person

The uniqueness is something absolute for the person and characterizes it. The person is so much absolute in its uniqueness that it does not allow itself to be added in other beings, to be used as a means, even for the most significant purpose.

It belongs indeed in the space of «mystery», the intentionality of this wonderful—however only «brushable» and not always visible—reality and in many cases, its interpretation. It becomes perceptible from those who have the possibility of «viewing» the other through an interior and intuitive look. The uniqueness of the person constitutes the internal «voice» of the entirety, the core of particularity and the creativity of human behavior (Kosmopoulos, 1990b).

A reality that its «whole» is not fixed by the sum of its natural and psychological parts and characteristics. A reality that does not indicate the closure of the soul in individualistic narcissism, neither comes in juxtaposition with the social tendency and behavior of the individual, because it is precisely the one that incorporates them in the service of so much personal and completely self-direction (that constitutes most basic possibility and energy of person's uniqueness) as much as it's universality and balance (Kosmopoulos, 1990b, 57).

Also, it is the one that can develop positively the social tendency in a way that it does not disturb the harmony and balance of the personality. Only the existence of the person constitutes the "safety valve" of the personality and it renders able to incorporate or even to transcend, the conflict between the individual and society. A reality that does not coincide with whatever psychology defined as *personality* or as *individuality*.

The uniqueness of the person in order to be comprehended and grow systematically in the schooling frames requires the existence of some social-educational preconditions. It cannot be appreciated and nourished by factors that nurtured in environments as familial, educational and social «camps», because neither of them conceived it, nor they felt its importance. Therefore, we understand the dangers that threaten particularly our tomorrow's world.

As it appears right now, it will be the world of "mass individual", because of that the international conformation movement of populations in strict-defined norms (mainly consuming, ideological etc.), as well as educative and land-planning mass societies and individuals, is not prevented in time. It cannot be nurtured from «unsuspecting» individuals, through their education, for the sense and value of the self or individuals with deep psychic traumas (Kosmopoulos, 1990b).

b. The Freedom of the Person

The development of the individual's freedom constitutes a basic trait of the personal situation. It is not only the development of the sense, but also the possibility of its applicability. It is mainly internal and multidimensional. The person feels that it can be autonomous, self-determined and self-ruled. Its life is open in experiences and changes. It lives literally the dynamics, it's *Relationaldynamics* existence with the self, the other and the nature: "as he becomes more fully himself, he will become more realistically socialized" (Rogers, 1961, p. 194). It feels free to follow its natural, organismic flow, but also that it has increased abilities to «transcend» it, whenever it needs. So, the person can extend itself and develop its sociability and its metaphysical dimension. As Victor Frankl, the creator of Logotherapy says: "…the true meaning of life is to be discovered in the world rather than within man or his own psyche, as though it were a closed system…The more one forgets himself—by giving himself to a cause to serve or another person to love—the more human he is and the more he actualizes himself. What is called self-actualization is not an attainable aim at all, for the simple reason that the more one would strive for it, the more he would miss it. In other words, self-actualization is possible only as a side-effect of self-transcendence" (Frankl, 1985b, p. 133).

The possibility of freedom and its multifaceted usage, testify the transcendental and «paradoxical» character of the person. The essential and harmonious cover of personality gaps, the transcendence of contradictions (or even «natural» antinomies), are fruits of the unified and dynamic expression of the person's freedom and responsibility. The transcendental potentiality of individualism and organismic levels of behavior revealed in a lot of cases, through the adoption of «paradoxical» behaviors. In these cases an «anarchic» behavior can be fruit of the person's conquered freedom and responsibility. Thus, it is possible not to contradict between them, the turn into the self and the turn into the Other, so much as attitude what as behavior.

c. The creativity and sociability of the person

The person's freedom of action, prompts the human being in creative attainments to itself and to the other. The internal freedom is expressed:

i. as liberation from impulsive urges, from the "conditions of
the authority.

ii. as responsible choice of the person in its effort to take a ▸
Greek), in the social environment.

The preceding is achieved by the acquisition of self-control, the configuration
of personal beliefs and the growing of autonomy. It is a creative process that has
direction towards the conquest of health and the plenitude of the person; this is
held in the psyche of the human being and very often, is also expressed in its
social behavior. The person prompted through the internal needs and forces
towards self-actualization, seeks each moment to be congruent with itself. For the
sake of this double ability that it has developed, it can be adapted in every environment and in every time, without sublime difficulties and without, also, end-
ing up to be a conformist. At the same time, its balance and maturity facilitate its
social behavior and makes it genuine, a fact that psychologically, constitutes condition for each essential social offer. The person in its effort to be moved to the
other without alienation, discovers it's tragedy but also the forces the beauty of its
personal existence, things that do not allow to wither its social impulse, obstacles
and disappointments (Kosmopoulos, 1990b).

The achievement of this goal is realised fast enough through the "view" of the
emerging, the developing person of the human being who confers, consults with
us for its topics. The emertion or the strengthening of the person imply in the
student emotions of happiness, high self-esteem and it increases vertically the certainty that with this step, with this movement that she has made—step and
movement probably dramatic—advanced for as never before in her self-actualization. Also, it increases its performance in each section of activity (Kosmopoulos,
1994).

Now we shall turn to a brief discussion of the phases and the stages of
Relationaldynamics learning model.

The Relationaldynamics Learning Model

The *Relationaldynamics* education of the person is developed in three basic
phases; the purpose of this education is fulfilled when the teacher reaches the
third phase.

In the first phase we observe the student's search and her "thirstiness" for completion and fullness. This need and desire make her move out of herself towards
the other or the strange. If the teacher has not the entire turn to the other, if she
does not try to discover the *person* of the younger other, she cannot move towards

ier student. If the student has not reached the existential feeling of the other and has not gone out for a loving search of her, then she can not make herself a fruitful field of the relationship, because she does not have the required "readiness", which is necessary for this kind of learning.

In the second phase the student—due to the appreciation and sympathy she feels for the teacher—is turned with favourable psychological disposition to everything that connects her with the teacher and teaching. The student—over the bridge of the developing relationship with her teacher—goes to a personal contact and meeting with the learning "good"; she can open her "gates" to knowledge without hesitation. Then, she will let the knowledge come selectively inside her and will let it operate according to her personal needs. By this way, she will take form (morphi ⇔ morphosis in Greek), be educated and, also, restore her *person* and fortify her renewing identity.

Last, in the third phase, the student's self is strengthened by the warm relationship with the teacher. She can separate gradually from the teacher. She is able to see the teacher realistically and as a human being (and not as the "superman" of yesterday) and can evaluate her in her real dimensions. The student can stand on her own feet and "fly" self-reliant towards the learning "good", to which she is connected directly and definitely. She even dares to dispute persons or knowledge. She expands her learning and educating potentialities in wider areas, as she is the only one responsible for her movements, she is self-educating. Now, the education is done, is fulfilled. The teacher can withdraw without guilt and hesitation. The student, as a new educated human being, comes to a state of self-knowledge and internal peace; then she can learn by herself and will not need the teacher anymore. The teacher experiences her own voluntary "death"; as a role she is self-abolished and finished.

The Relationaldynamics Learning Model
Phase A:
TEACHER'S ADAPTATION TO THE CLASSROOM AND TO EVERY STUDENT—PREPARATION-
(Climate of "frugality", ease, joy and acceptance).

1

We are careful of our initial attitude and position towards the children in the classroom. Relationships of respect, trust, freedom and responsibility.

↓

2

We explore and cultivate the *Relationaldynamics* potentiality of the schooling frame (administrative briefing, relationships with the director and the colleagues). We are strongly interested in the function of the school as a "community" and, inside it, in the function of the student-councils per class.

↓

3

We are informed about the student's family, friends and social environment. We estimate her learning possibilities and needs.

↓

4

We trace each student's learning interests, needs, potentialities and abilities. We provide to each one of them possibilities to succeed.

Phase B:
THE TEACHER FACILITATES THE STUDENT'S EFFORT TO COME IN A DIRECT EDUCATING RELATIONSHIP WITH THE LEARNING "GOOD".

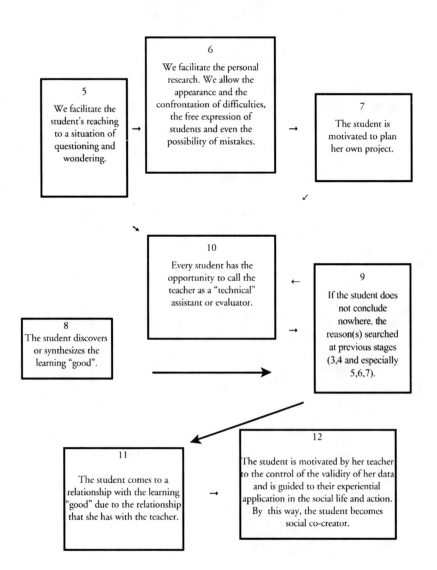

PHASE C:
THE STUDENT REMAINS IN RELATIONSHIP WITH THE LEARNING "GOOD".
THE TEACHER WITHDRAWS.

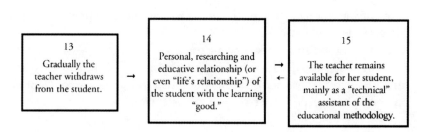

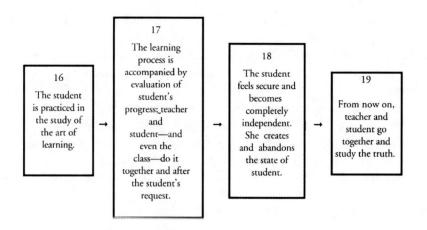

Commentary

From the preceding we understand that we need a policy which genuinely believes in the outcomes of modern education, psychology and sociology and allows the school to become a cultural institution, having the scientific certainty that the graduates will succeed and will become healthy and happy individuals.

Giving priority:

- to the psychoeducational culture of everyone who is involved in the learning process.
- to the organization of the school and the educational system with these perceptions (decentralization).
- to the inspiration and support of the teacher.
- to another regard of education and the teacher. The *Relationaldynamics* functioning of the teacher isn't something that can result randomly or simply through her experience but through systematic training.

The education of the future must be person-centered and in the heart of this education are the dynamics of relationship and the school of the person that as an educative area, has an anthropocentric role. Today it is positive the fact that we talk about a "turn into the person" and a re-discovery of the person, that is not limited of course in the field of education. Winfried Bφhm (1998), from a philosophical view, states that towards the "modern intellectual situation" and the "educational demands of the new century", the goal of education owes to be the "the human person" (292). Certainly person-centered education places high requirements both for the teacher and the student, as well as in the quality of their relationship. According to Bφhm the suspiciousness, with which the education of the person is faced by a lot of educators, is owed in the fact that it requires maturity and creativity from the part of the teacher, in whom it does not offer ready directions for the educational action, proposing instead its «character» as a risk and adventure (1998, 298-299). The research and scientific experiences all over the world, demonstrate that only this kind of school is capable of being effective and having the educational ability to prepare the citizen of the 21st century and the universal person. The school is able to grant the societies of tomorrow with graduates capable of metabolizing information into knowledge, skills and abilities important to their person, which is developing through its education. And as Rogers used to say money has to be invested into the person's inner power (Rogers, & Freiberg, 1994, 166), the power of the student and the power of the teacher as persons, during all levels or forms of education, in which everyone is considered to be an active agent and participant in her own formative work. Supporting such a school is a long breath reformation and a tranquil lasting revolution.

Another paper further explaining *Relationaldynamics* education and tracing its similarities and differences with Rogers's Person-Centered approach to education is planned for the future.

Grigoris Mouladoudis, PhD (University of Patras), is a psychologist and person-centered group facilitator. He is adjunct lecturer of educational psychology at the Department of Primary Education, University of Ioannina, Greece.

Alexandros Kosmopoulos, PhD (University of Paris, Sorbonne), is an educationist, psychologist philosopher, and the creator of *Relationaldynamics* (Shesiodynamici) as a Humanistic, person-centered approach for Education and Counseling. He is professor at the *Department of Education, University of Patras, Greece.*

REFERENCES

Allport, G. (1968). *The person in psychology*. Boston: Beacon Press.

Böhm, W. (1998). Das Subjekt ist tot. Es lebe die Person. *Pädagogische Rundschau*, 52, 291-301.

Buber, M. (1958). *I and thou* (2nd ed., R. G. Smith, Trans.). New York: Charles Scribner's Sons.

Buber, M.(1963). *Israel and the world: Essays in a time of crisis*. New York: Schocken.

Buber, M. (1965a). *Between man and man*. (R. G. Smith, Trans.). New York: Macmillan.

Buber, M. (1965b). *The knowledge of man: A philosophy of the interhuman* (M. Friedman & R. G. Smith, Trans.). New York: Harper & Row.

Caruso, I. (1964). *Existential psychology: From analysis to synthesis*. (E. Krapf, Trans.). New York: Herder and Herder.

Combs, A. (1988). Is there a future for humanistic or person-centered education? In C. B. Hansen, & F., Nell Roebuck, (Eds.), The person-centered approach in education (special issue). *Person-Centered Review*, 3 (1), 96-103.

DeCarvalho, R. (1991). The humanistic paradigm in education. *The Humanistic Psychologist*, 19(1), 88-104.

Frankl, V. (1985a). *Psychotherapy and existentialism: Selected papers on logotherapy*. Simon and Schuster: New York.

Frankl, V. (1985b). *Man's search for meaning*. New York: Simon and Schuster.

Giorgi, A. (1995). Phenomenological psychology. In J.A. Smith, R. Harre, and L. van Langenhove (Eds.), *Rethinking psychology* (pp. 24-42). London: Sage Publications.

Hill, J. (1994). *Person-centred approaches in schools*. Manchester: PCCS.

Kosmopoulos, A. (1990a). *Shesiodynamici Pedagogiki tou Prosopou* (2nd ed.). [Relationaldynamics Education of the Person]. Athens: Grigoris.

Kosmopoulos, A. (1990b). *To sholio pethan: Zito to sholio tou prosopou!* [The School is dead. Viva the School of the Person!] Athens: Grigoris.

Kosmopoulos, A. (1994). *Psychologia kai odigitiki tis paidikis kai neanikis ilikias* [Psychology and guidance of the childhood and adolescence]. Athens: Grigoris.

Maslow, A. (1987). *Motivation and personality* (3rd ed.). New York: Harper & Row.

Merleau-Ponty, M. (1976). *Phenomenologie de la perception*. Paris: Gallimard.

Mouladoudis, G. (2001). Dialogical psychotherapy and person-centered approach to therapy: Beyond correspondences and contrasts toward a fertile interconnection, *The Person-Centered Journal, 8*(1-2), 4-15.

Mouladoudis, G. & Patrikiou, D. (2002). Person-centered approach to counseling and Greek-Orthodox Christian Church: Tentative tracing of their parallel paths and exploration of potential encounter between them.

Mounier, E. (1952). *Personalism*. (P. Mairet, Trans.). London: Routledge & K. Paul.

Patterson, C. & Hidore, S. (1997). The goal: Self-actualizing persons. In *Successful psychotherapy: A caring, loving relationship* (pp. 53-67). Northvale: Aronson.

Richards, A., & Combs, A. (1992). Education and the humanistic challenge. In F J. Wertz (Ed.), *The humanistic movement: Recovering the person in psychology* (pp.256-273). New York: Gardner.

Rogers, C. (1961). *On becoming a person*. Boston: Houghton Mifflin.

Rogers, C. (1969). *Freedom to learn* (1st ed.). Columbus: Merill.

Rogers, C. (1970). *Encounter groups*. Middlesex: Penguin.

Rogers, C. (1980). *A way of being*. Boston: Houghton Mifflin.

Rogers, C. (1983). *Freedom to learn for the 80s* (2nd ed.). Columbus: Charles Merrill.

Rogers, C. & Freiberg, J. (1994). *Freedom to learn* (3rd ed.). New York: Merrill.

Rose, J. (2001). Editorial, *The Person-Centered Journal, 8*(1-2),

Rogers, C. & Schmid, P. (1998). Person–zentriert. Grundlagen von Theorie und Praxis (3rd ed.). Mainz: Grónewald.

Schmid, P. (1998). On becoming a person-centred approach: A person-centred understanding of the Person. In B. Thorne, & E. Lambers (Eds.), *Person-centred therapy: European perspectives* (pp. 38-52). London: Sage.

Spinelli, E. (1989). *The interpreted world: An introduction to phenomenological psychology*. London: Sage.

Wertz, E J. (1992). (Ed.). *The humanistic movement: Recovering the person in psychology*. New York: Gardner.

Person-Centered Supervision:
An Experiential Perspective

Doug Bower

As a result of a pilgrimage into the arena of pastoral counseling, and later a journey into the realms of professional counseling, I became convinced that supervision is extremely important in becoming a counselor/therapist. My initial experience was in Clinical Pastoral Education at Emory University Hospital in Atlanta, GA. While that experience was not directly related to pastoral counseling, it was an experience of self-examination and confrontation that set the stage for my movement into counseling. I regard that experience as quite rewarding and growthful.

Yet, I don't recommend C.P.E. to people any more. My philosophy changed and I fail now to appreciate the in-your-face style of the model I was exposed to. As I reflect back on the experience, I remember taking C.P.E. for me and was thus free from meeting the requirements of a seminary or ordination process. I think that freedom allowed it to be growthful. I could work on my personal and professional growth free of grades and external conditions.

I recall my supervisor, Chuck Carpenter, using me as his presentation for qualifying for supervisor status with ACPE (the Association of Clinical Pastoral Education). He was one of the few people who got his credentials on the first attempt. However, for several weeks he playfully harassed me for almost causing him to fail his examine. Apparently, he was accused of being too nice to me.

Frankly, that was what I wanted. I wanted a supervisor who trusted me enough to grow without attempting to beat me up in the name of therapeutic confrontation. Other supervisors in that C.P.E. experience were far more confrontational. Yet, I believe because they had no particular power in my life, I was inconvenienced by the confrontations, but not overwhelmed by the fear that their confrontations could hurt me academically, or my ordination process. Thus,

I was able to engage the confrontations more constructively. I don't want to explain that further.

Shortly, after completing C.P.E., I began studying pastoral counseling. A significant part of that experience was the supervision. Between, 1981 to 1985, I was engaged in supervision. It was both an individual experience and a peer group experience which I enjoyed very much until I attempted to get out. Then it turned sour.

When I entered pastoral counseling, I had a strong interest in a psychodynamic approach to psychotherapy. I actually fancied myself as being able to analyze people with ease.

In 1983, I stumbled across an opportunity to begin studies for a Ph.D. in counseling at the University of Georgia. I had moved to Athens after being appointed to Oconee Street United Methodist Church. I thought it would be a great idea to pick up courses at the university to transfer to the Th.M. program in pastoral counseling I was working on. What I didn't expect was discovering the Person-Centered Approach in the process.

I took a theories of counseling and psychotherapy course with Jerold Bozarth which allowed me to make a discovery that was to change my view of counseling and psychotherapy. I had heard of Carl Rogers for years and had dabbled a bit in his theory, but it didn't click with me. Studying with Jerold Bozarth changed that in that I was studying with someone who was an adherent of the approach, not just a teacher of the approach from another orientation.

I continued getting supervision in pastoral counseling. But I was also receiving supervision from the University of Georgia. The latter gave me the opportunity to expand my horizons, but also gave me ammunition in my stubbornness to stick up for what I strongly believed. In 1985, I had completed all the requirements for the Th.M. save one, the final examination from the supervisory component. I had satisfactorily completed every term, and it was time to get out.

However, in attempting to present my growing and developing understanding of the person-centered approach I was failed by the examination community. The pastoral counseling program had a long history of making it difficult for people to get out of their graduate programs. My own advisor had allegedly failed his final examinations six times in regards to his Doctor of Sacred Theology (S.T.D).

I was excited by what I had discovered and pleased with what I had learned and was ready to get out of the program. Since I was no longer psycho-dynamically oriented, I felt it would be unethical to attempt to apply this theory to my practicum presentation. So I chose to use the person-centered approach since I was confident with it, developing a broader network with it, and could use its jargon.

To my dismay (but not to my surprise), I hit a brick wall. I was incensed and beside myself that I too had been treated like other students had been treated. My recollection is now tainted by many years of distance from the episode, but I recall being failed for not providing a client I had seen at least fifteen times, for not providing an extensive psycho-dynamic style psycho-social history, and for not getting into the client's sexual history.

Instead, I had used a modified Barrett-Lennard Relationship Inventory (Powell, 1977), and addressed the case from the person-centered approach asking if I had been successful at achieving high levels of empathy, genuineness, and acceptance. According to the client, to my self assessment, and to the Relationship Inventory, I had been successful. Most of all the client and I were able to give an accounting of the client's growth and change during a nine week therapy experience. Why nine weeks? We had eliminated about six to seven weeks of doing that extensive psycho-social history required by the psycho-dynamic model.

I gave up that degree since I was working on a Ph.D. anyway. It has been both a regret because I worked hard for that degree, but a source of satisfaction in that I did not compromise my integrity just to get a degree. I stuck with that in which I believed, being person-centered. I now consider it unethical to attempt to utilize a theoretical approach to counseling in which one does not believe.

Though my exit experience from the pastoral counseling experience was a negative one, I did leave believing in supervision. I believe in long term supervision though not a career-long supervision as espoused by Borders & Usher (1992). At some point, a counselor has to grow up and take the keys to the car. Supervisory consultations seem very appropriate and a humorous one can be found in the beginning of Malone & Whitaker's (1981) work, "The Roots of Psychotherapy."

Nearly, 12 years later I was asked to help Fort Valley State University in the counseling psychology department. I was initially asked to teach the Community Mental Health class, but was also given the Mental Health Counseling Internship.

The internship was in disarray and in the first term I had difficulty even finding out who the students were in the course. Since, I hadn't initially agreed to supervise students, I wasn't in a position to augment my own schedule to provide the students with weekly meetings. In their naivete and mine, the students did not receive adequate contact with a campus supervisor. Fortunately, each intern had an onsite supervisor and did receive adequate contact from them.

By the end of the term, we had corrected that and made it possible for students to begin getting good learning experiences through weekly peer group meetings with individual supervision being provided for by on-site supervisors.

As far as I am concerned the program was loaded with examples of a need to provide better opportunities for supervision experiences. The chief among these was the need for audio taping with clients. However, I did not initially get the support I needed from the department to change that. The local agencies which agreed to offer the interns counseling experiences kept refusing to allow the students to tape clients. They were concerned about breaches in confidentiality. Even though I kept assuring people that we were bound by the same ethics about confidentiality that the agencies were, this did not solve the problem. I also kept trying to ask, "If you think that a breach of confidentiality can be a problem, what kinds of problems would you have for incompetence concerning counselors who were not trained properly?" That didn't help either.

Fortunately, a full time faculty member with daily contact with the department took over the internship for one term. Unfortunately, that faculty member abruptly left after getting taping instilled into the program. With this sudden change, I was once again contacted to provide supervision. I was excited that taping was part of the supervision experience. It allowed for a better look at what students were doing with clients.

Purposes of Supervision

Freeman & McHenry (1996) offered five goals related to supervision. 1) Help the supervisee gain deeper self-awareness. 2) Help the supervisee understand client perceptions. 3) Help the supervisee develop the skills needed for counseling/psychotherapy. 4) Offer the supervisee a supportive setting for learning. 5) Model parts of the counseling process in the supervision process.

The above jargon is not totally consistent with the person-centered approach, but it is far from being inconsistent either. I believe the person-centered approach is more than capable of meeting these goals. It would be a matter of holding the principles of the person-centered approach and facilitating the growth of the supervisee. In this, the person-centered supervisor would not direct the process.

To strengthen the internship experiences I offered students several opportunities. First, there would be case presentations based on the instruments of the agencies. "Supervision may include, without being limited to, review of case presentations, audio tapes, videotapes, and direct observation of the practitioners clinical skills" (Rules, 2002). As I pointed out, initial regional agency resistance made it virtually impossible to review audio and videotapes. There was a consistent expression of concern over breach of confidentiality. Even though I assured agency directors that we were subject to the same ethical guidelines as the agency was, no one would allow taping. The agencies were afraid of being sued. Even when asked what it would be like to be sued for incompetency because the student was not prepared, the agency directors still balked at taping.

Thus we were initially limited to the review of case presentations which included presenting the intake protocols, reports from psychological tests performed by psychologists, and a variety of progress notes.

If the interns were given opportunities to present didactic material to their clientele, which might include local schools and other local agencies, in addition to center activities with clients and groups, they were allowed to use these experiences as part of their internship presentations. We often found these quite informative about trends in the mental-health treatment community.

My experience of virtually all the scenarios from the local agencies whether they be state or nonprofit was that the models are far more consistent with managed-care and treatment modalities than the person-centered approach. This was fine as it was not my intent to create person-centered clones according to the stereotypes held by Doug Bower. Rather I was interested in discovering what I could about all these different treatment philosophies as well as facilitating the intern's experience with mental-health realities that were not consistent with my own hopes and dreams about what mental-health should be. I of course am prejudice toward the person-centered model. However I am very much aware that my students in the agencies which they served cannot use nor perhaps even like the person centered model. Therefore, it seemed much more appropriate to let the student be his/her own best expert concerning how to grasp the model he or she was exposed to in the agency that offered the training. In the process, I learned a great deal about the present state of mental health care, one thing of which is that it changes quite frequently. Intake protocols, progress notes, services, and the rules and regulations of the centers were consistently changing.

All in all I was quite satisfied that the students were consistently growing and developing as budding professionals in the counseling arena.

Second, students were expected to read articles from peer reviewed journals on counseling and psychotherapy issues. This was later enhanced with readings from texts on counseling. Lest this sound directive, I needed an objective criteria for giving grades. The students were not told what articles to read though I couldn't justify accepting Dr. Johnson's Web Site on Depression as an example of graduate work. The topics and journals were selected by the students who amazed me with the integrity of their findings.

Third, with the internship being two semesters in length we alternated between the Rules and Regulations for the State of Georgia, and the ethics of the American Counseling Association. This gave the interns a look at what the state government, and a professional association would expect of them. In this, I made no determination of what they should know. I simply presented the material.

The Basic Premisses of Person-Centered Supervision

A Basic Trust

It has been a long held belief of those espousing the person-centered approach that people have vast capacities for growth and change. Rogers (1942) said, "It will be evident that the approach of the non-directive group applies to the overwhelming majority of clients who have the capacity to achieve reasonably adequate solutions for their problems. Counseling, from this viewpoint, cannot be the only method for dealing with that small group—the psychotic, the defective, and perhaps some others—who have not the capacity to solve their own difficulties, even with help" (p. 128). At that point Rogers saw a limitation on this capacity for change to a small population of clients. This small group of clients was made up of non-chronic and mildly troubled persons.

However, by the end of his career this view expanded. Rogers (1980) wrote, "individuals have within themselves vast resources for self-understanding and for altering their self-concepts, basic attitudes, and self-directed behavior; these resources can be tapped if a definable climate of facilitate psychological attitudes can be provided" (p.115). He didn't limit this to a handful of clients, but to all kinds of clients with all kinds of personal struggles. Thus a college student getting over a failed romance could change, but so could a person with a severe mental disability. While Rogers didn't assert that the severely mentally disabled would become "normal," he did espouse that even the people caught in the most severe of human problems would change when conditions were present to facilitate the change. Certainly Rogers's later position allowed for the uniqueness of change in given populations and with given problems.

This same trust can be applied to students in training (Magnuson, Norem, & Wilcoxon, 2000). Magnuson et al, emphasized this trust in the sense of forming rapport with supervisees. He has the feeling of cordiality. The twist of the person-centered approach would include this aspect of rapport but add that supervisees have a wide variety of resources for growing toward professional and personal goals during training.

As far as I am concerned a major issue is putting so much trust in the ability to change that the supervisor takes a laissez faire attitude. Let me illustrate. A dialogue began on the cct/pca Internet network in which the chief issue was whether or not a cct/pca counselor should answer questions from the client. Two apparent camps developed. One camp said, no. To answer the question would be too directive. The other camp said, yes. I lean heavily to the latter camp. If I am asked a question and I have an answer, I'll share it. I am open to the client's disagreement with my answer and try not to present my answer as the only answer.

Since in the supervisor's use of the person-centered approach the supervisor is transparent, the supervisee gets a glimpse of the beliefs of the supervisor and is trusted to deal with those beliefs. Certainly the interns at Fort Valley State had a variety of questions, some of which I knew and some of which I did not. Whether I have an answer or not, I attempt to communicate that I was not and am not a walking encyclopedia on anything. There are even things about my own life I have forgotten. So I don't try to snow students with the attitude that I am the expert. I had a professor in seminary whom I respected greatly who reminded me that he was the professor and I was the student. His answer was always right. As his student, I would say, "yes sir." As his colleague, I would confront him with his audacity and mine.

Magnuson et al (2000) hold there are four aspects of supervisory concern which I believe are applicable to the issue of laissez-faire. Person-centered supervisors cannot ignore them in the name of trusting the supervisee. These are 1) vicarious liability—whereby the supervisor has been assigned "ultimate responsibility" for what the supervisee does or doesn't do. 2) Confidentiality—it goes without saying that what the client shares with the supervisee who in turn shares it in supervision stays in the room unless of course it falls under the legal domain of "duty to inform." 3) Dual relationships—supervisors are not to exploit supervisees sexually, economically, or by providing therapy to supervisees. On the latter, I disagree on one hand. The supervisory relationship is often an intimate and revealing relationship. Given the attitudinal qualities offered by the approach and its inherent position of putting the client in charge of his/her growth, one would have a difficult time arguing this is a problem in person-centered supervision, unless of course a person absolutely was subjectively aghast at the idea of providing therapy and supervision to the same person. Yet, even as I write in disagreement I have never provided both therapy and supervision to the same individual. On the other hand, I would completely agree that sex with supervisees or entering into economic endeavors with supervisees is unethical and out of place in the supervisory relationship. Finally, 4) Power differential—there is the danger that supervisors can abuse this power with bullying, coercing, and intimidation.

Perhaps all four of these can be seen in the power and authority of the stereotype of the "expert."

To Give up the Role of Expert

A stereotype of an expert is one who knows the answers. The problem though with this model is the vast expanse of knowledge. No one person can know all the answers. Even within disciplines to attempt to maintain an image of knowing all the answers is futile as there is too much to know. I watched a television interview on genetic engineering in which the "expert" answered every single question posed to him often referring to the literature and to his own research concerning DNA. As I watched, there was a host of material that I disagreed with or questioned. The point is not that I disagreed, but that one individual can only assimilate so much information and be exposed to but a small section of the world. Another person may discover other information which contradicts the observations of others. Thus, an "expert" really needs to be constantly exploring as new information changes views. I have long observed that if you get a room full of experts on a subject the disagreement will be so extensive that it would be difficult to keep up with all the points of disagreement.

In the realm of the psychotherapeutic community, the stereotypical role of the expert is being able to determine what is wrong with the client. Since the client is too close to the problem, or being controlled by unconscious aspects of his or her personality, the therapist is in the best position to determine what is wrong with the client.

This is extended further in that since the client cannot really know what is wrong with him/her, then the therapist can't really expect that the client can fix the problem. Thus, the expert therapist treats the client with methodologies too complex for the average client to understand, let alone use. So the expert is one who can propose fixes for the client, or that the client can use to fix him or her self (Rogers, 1977).

In supervision, the beginning intern in this "expert" model has to be guided, directed, and given the correct answers by the supervisor. The supervisor then has the answers, and knows what to say in the circumstances before the intern knows.

I had a couple of supervisors in my training experience that fit the "expert" stereotype pretty well. When I resisted, I was confronted with being anti-authoritarian. I of course would feel guilty, but still not necessarily cooperate. And that tended to be the base of a criticism of me, "you aren't doing what I say do, so you have trouble with authority figures." While I have seen a variety of helping professionals whom I believe have met the stereo-type, I also have witnessed their denial in assuming such a role. In expressing my observations, my concerns were simply seen as resistance.

The person-centered approach rejects this stereo-type. "This newer approach differs from the older one in that it has a genuinely different goal. It aims directly toward a greater independence and integration of the individual rather than hoping that such results will accrue if the counselor assists in solving the problem...The aim is not to solve one particular problem but to assist the individual to grow, so that he can cope with the present problem and with later problems in a better integrated fashion" (Rogers, 1977, p. 6).

Addressing the "politics" of the helping professions Rogers (1977) wrote, "Politics, in present-day psychological and social usage, has to do with power and control; with the extent to which persons desire, attempted to obtain, possess, share, or surrender power control over others and/or themselves. It has to do with the maneuvers, the strategies and tactics, witting or unwitting, by which such power and control over one's own life and others' lives is sought and gained–and were shared or relinquished. It has to do with the locus of decision-making power: who makes the decisions which, consciously or unconsciously, regulate or control the thoughts, feelings, or behavior of others or oneself" (p. 4).

The person-centered therapist gives up the role of the expert and the traditional authority that goes with it (Bower, 1985) "Adherence to client-centered theory then depends upon the extent to which the therapist is willing to give up and/or the client is able to overcome the 'interfering interventions' which are posed to the client" (Bozarth, 1995, p. 16). The client is his/her own "best expert."

In translating this to supervision, the person-centered supervisor gives up his/her role as expert determining what is best for the supervisee and the supervisee's client. In person-centered supervision, the supervisor expects that the student is quite capable of identifying problems, situations, and issues in therapy. It has been my experience that the beginning supervisee may have trouble articulating those observations in relationship to theories, practice, and client interactions, but as he or she continues to engage clients on a regular basis, the ability to say what is happening in the counseling—therapeutic setting improves.

Yet, I, as the supervisor, have become one of the intern's resources. To sit passively by and deny my students what I do know or don't know deprives them of resources. This is not a laissez faire model. It is a model of trust which requires the active participation of the therapist or in this case the supervisor.

A Basic Genuineness in the Supervisor

I have already alluded above to the transparency of the supervisor. I don't believe that depriving or withholding information, thoughts, reactions, ideas, or observations is congruent with what it means to be person-centered. The supervisee should be able to see right through the supervisor concerning matters of supervision. This is of course figurative of the supervisee being able to know something of the feelings, experiences, and thoughts of the supervisor.

It is important that the supervisor not hide beyond a facade of aloofness and objectivity, but that he or she be open to the supervisor/supervisee relationship and all that it entails. I am not making a case for the supervisor letting the supervisee in on every detail. But I do believe that the supervisor in the person-centered approach exercises a "when appropriate" stance concerning his or her experiences and feelings, etc., in the relationship.

A Basic Acceptance by the Supervisor

I completely reject the notion of unconditional positive regard. It is not the positive regard that is at issue for me, it is the word "unconditional." I cannot make a case of acceptance being unconditional. I can only make a case of the presence of acceptance.

In this state of acceptance the supervisor accepts the supervisee at the level he or she is functioning. That doesn't mean that the supervisor looks the other way when unethical behavior appears, or incompetency is discovered. The genuine therapist has to determine an appropriate response to therapeutic deviations that may reflect unethical or incompetent practice.

It does mean that the budding therapist is not expected to make timely, appropriate, or well informed responses in relationship of the supervisee in relationship with the client.

A Basic Understanding by the Supervisor

In this the same "entering the world as if" (Rogers, 1942, 1977, & 1980) quality is practiced by the supervisor. The situation is the only change. Instead of therapy, this is supervision. The supervisor thus attempts to see the world of the supervisee as it is seen by the supervisee.

An additional element is appropriate. The supervisor needs also to see the world of the client as the client sees it. I like to take notes during the hearing of tapes writing down what I have learned about the client.

I also like to make the same observations concerning the supervisee for I should be able to learn something about the supervisee as well.

A Basic Application in the Internship Peer Group Experience

Theory

I have found that dealing with theory has gotten difficult in relationship to the mechanics of the managed care model. I often say to people when I discuss managed care that the model has discovered the key to therapeutic growth. It is not theory, and it is not technique or relationships. It is paper work and filling out forms. The more redundant the forms, the more therapeutic.

I believe the supervisee is more than capable of deciding on which theory he or she uses. One student may be interested in a modified Psychoanalytic/developmental model. Another may like Reality Therapy. My experience with supervisees is that most are rather eclectic having been exposed to a variety of theories in their Counseling and Theories class, but not being exposed to any long term training in any one theory.

Certainly during the discussing of clients, issues of theory emerge.

Practice

I am rather concerned that the supervisees are not being offered a course on Helping Relationships or interpersonal relationship at Fort Valley State. It is like they are thrown into deep waters to sink or swim without being given swimming lessons. To date, all the students have survived this toss into the sea. Again with so much focus on forms and paper work, the sites providing the supervisees with opportunities to learn aren't really concerned with counseling skills. They want the forms filled out properly.

As the internship progresses, supervisees seem to have been able to assimilate counseling skills as they gain more confidence and become more efficient at gathering the information for the paper work. This enables them to find more occasions for interacting with clients and thus have more interpersonal contact with them.

Evaluation

I use a point system of evaluation. I make no attempt to judge the students. I only use the criteria of whether the supervisee turns in materials.

I offer points for every article or chapter of the internship text that they read and report. I ask only for peer reviewed articles, most of which are plucked off the Internet via Galileo. I do discourage visiting Dr. So & So's Website on depression and getting Web page materials. The articles have been awesome. I read all the articles and put them into a bibliography to give to the students and faculty members.

I also give points for the site supervisor's evaluation form and the supervisor's confirmation of the supervisee's client contact hours. I honor what the supervisee and the supervisor have worked out in terms of those contacts.

Finally, supervisees get points for presentations. I don't give points based on the quality of the presentation. Since supervisees are functioning at different levels, I don't find it helpful to grade presentations. Being freed of the fear of having their work graded, I have found that the supervisees present some very puzzling and baffling cases. The presentations represent deep struggles with very complicated problems.

While I don't grade, I do ask questions. I most often want to know what makes a supervisee make certain conclusions about a client. For instance, if a supervisee states that the client has a problem because of some developmental problem between the age of 1 to 3 years of age, I might very well ask why the supervisee believes that. I want to know if the student knows what he or she is talking about.

Further, peer group interaction becomes quite intense during many presentations. I haven't seen anyone be self righteous or act with an air of superiority in these interactions, but rather with thoughtful consideration of the issues.

Helping the Client through Person-Centered Supervision of the Intern

I am not in a position to defend the following claim with research. What I am about to say is a hypothesis based on my observation. My claim is that as the supervisor participates in the growth and development of the supervisee, the clients are indirectly helped. In part, this position emerges from witnessing counseling experiences with individuals who sought marital counseling with me, but whose spouses refused to participate in counseling. I often found that as clients grew, their marriages improved. That growth included observations of 1) growing confidence, 2) a greater interest in perceiving the world of the absent spouse as that spouse sees it, 3) an increase in the level of acceptance of the absent spouse, and 4) a greater willingness to allow the relationship to move in any direction rather than in a direction that matched preconceived expectations about what a good marriage should look like. I consequently saw a variety of marriages rescued even though I personally reached a point as a therapist that I was convinced the couple would soon get a divorce.

In relationship to my claim, I have often been amazed that the supervisees are often an oasis in their clients' lives and that the supervisees were quite helpful to their clients in some very helpless and powerless situations. As the growth of the supervisees was facilitated, so was their ability to help facilitate the growth of clients.

Ethics

Personally, I see the person-centered approach as very ethical though not in the legalistic sense. There are no specific rules on confidentiality, etc. The ethics arise through the respect of the client and putting the client first.

However, the ethics of the profession cannot be ignored and the supervisees I have supervised are not adopting the person-centered approach. Further, licensure requirements include exposure to professional ethical standards. Thus, it is important that the supervisees have an opportunity to see ethical guidelines. Every other semester, I pass out copies of the ethical guidelines of the American Counseling Association. I then present those in brief didactic form and commentary at the begin of the peer group seminar until we have completed the guidelines.

This generally produces a lot of discussion and questions. The dilemmas the supervisees raise are often baffling and complex. They often generate more discussion on the ethical issues than through the case presentation material.

Criticism of the Person-Centered Approach to Supervision

Davenport (1992) reviewing an interview with C.H. Patterson decided that person-centered supervision is almost unethical. "Client-centered supervision, appealing as it may be, fails to meet the rigorous ethical and legal guidelines now required of counselor supervisors" (p. 227).

Magnuson, Wilcoxon, Norem, (2000) presented several categories of "lousy supervision" which can be used to determine if person-centered supervision could indeed fail to meet "ethical and legal guidelines" for the contemporary supervisor: unbalanced, developmentally inappropriate, intolerant of differences, poor model of professional/personal attributes, untrained, professionally apathetic, organizational/administrative (fail to establish parameters, and technical/cognitive (unskilled and unreliable).

Is person-centered supervision unbalanced? Since the focus is on the supervisee in relationship with the supervisor it cannot be. Supervisees bring in different knowledge based on cognitive and experiential phenomena. In addition, the settings in which they provide counseling and care often use models of care that are quite different from the approach of the person-centered supervisor. Thus, the supervisor will grow when he/she encounters these other perspectives.

In turn, the supervisor also has a vast treasure of experiences. Supervision would be unbalanced if the supervisor simply responded stereo-typically by saying "yes ah-huh" or repeating the last thing the supervisee says. If the supervisor illustrates, shares, and makes comments based on his/her experience within the frame of the attitude of acceptance, empathy, and genuineness, supervision will not be unbalanced, save for the limitations of the supervisor's experience.

Is person-centered supervision developmentally inappropriate? No, it cannot be or the supervisor is not practicing person-centered supervision. Since the supervisor is interested in discovering where the supervisee is on a variety of cognitive and experiential domains, the supervisor always attempts to get at the appropriate developmental place of the supervisee. In this, there is a basic belief that this will change in some way as the supervisee gains experience in counseling.

Is the person-centered supervisor intolerant of differences? Since this approach emphasizes empathy, and understanding, its high regard for diversity makes this a nonissue except that an individual therapist may fail to practice the approach.

Is the person-centered approach a poor model of professional/personal attributes? As of this writing, the theory and its practice has undergone scrutiny for nearly sixty years. It has been found valid by some and it has been found of no value by others as well. It has been accepted and rejected. In all this it has withstood the test of scrutiny. It is a model of compassion and care which focuses heavily upon the client or supervisee. It is doubtful that any one would accuse the model as not being a caring model, though there are those who would be adamant that the conditions are not sufficient for a lot of circumstances, among them would be Wolberg (1977).

Are person-centered supervisors untrained? Like all the other theoretical orientations a person has to start somewhere. Georgia law (Rules, 2002a) offers several guidelines concerning supervision. This is consistent with Mangusus et al (2000) claim that 45 states require pre-licensing, post-graduate supervision. Certainly, this principle can be violated, but those who provide person-centered supervision would be trained in providing the core conditions and have experience in using them. The transition to supervision would not be all that great in moving from counseling to supervision. The focus changes from personal growth to professional growth. The shift is one of facilitating the emergence of the self that one truly is to facilitating the therapist that one truly is.

Is the person-centered approach subject to allowing one to be professionally apathetic? Surely, any given individual could be accused of being apathetic. However, the person-centered approach requires a great deal of concentration. Apathy does not facilitate the core conditions needed in person-centered supervision.

Does the person-centered supervisor fail to establish parameters? I think the passive stereo-type of the model can. I have long felt that the approach is too permissive and condones behavior rather than being empathic about behavior. However, the real parameters of person-centered supervision are based on the theory and practice of the approach. Therefore, person-centered therapy cannot be without parameters. The emphasis though is upon the resourcefulness of the supervisee in relationship to the client and the supervisor and of course the work setting.

Are person-centered supervisors unskilled and unreliable? The approach is about being skilled in offering empathy, understanding, and genuineness. The belief is that the supervisee can grow professionally if these attitudinal qualities are presented on a persistent and consistent basis.

I find Davenport's charge about client-centered therapy failing to meet rigorous ethical and legal guidelines unfounded and undefendable. I have never heard from my first class of interns concerning acknowledgment of their success at getting licenses. I started hearing from other classes though as their awareness became heightened as to the requirements for licensure and they could focus on what they needed to do to qualify for licensure. I do not know what the success rate of the students I have supervised is. While, I believe that supervision is a part of the preparation for licensure, it is not designed to help students pass licensure exams. It is part of facilitating the supervisee to grow as a potential counselor/therapist.

Conclusion

While I interacted with a variety of sources concerning person-centered supervision of counseling students, I am relying heavily on my experience. That experience has led me to believe that the person-centered approach is a viable and valuable discipline for providing supervision. It is extremely flexible and allows for the individuality of supervisees. Further, it does not impose presuppositions upon the student, but only an attitude.

The main interest of my application of the approach is to facilitate the growth of the student. I have no idea what direction the student will take, but have found each one I have observed to grow in presentations and knowledge. However, in this, I make no claim to get the student into a position to pass a licensing exam. I do, though, claim to affirm the experiential requirements for licensure. The standards for that though are established by the university while it keeps in mind the requirements for licensure in Georgia. To date I know of no student who was denied a license because of lack of experience with clients.

I am simply affirming in this work that the person-centered approach is a significant framework for being with supervisees as they prepare to become counselors.

I also affirm that I put my own unique twist to what it means to be a person providing person-centered supervision.

REFERENCES

Borders, L. D., & Usher, C. H. (1992). Post-degree supervision: Existing and preferred practices. *Journal of Counseling & Development*, 70 (5), 594-599.

Bower, D. W. (1985). The assumptions and attitudes of the Rogerian person-centered approach: Implications for pastoral counseling. Unpublished Research Project.

Bozarth, J. D. (1995). Person-centered therapy: A misunderstood paradigmatic difference? *The Person-Centered Journal*, 2(2), 12-17.

Davenport, D.S. (1992). Ethical and legal problems with client-centered supervision. *Counselor Education & Supervision*, 31 (4), 227-231.

Freeman, B., & ; McHenry, S. (1996). Clinical supervision of counselors-in-training: A nationwide survey of ideal delivery, goals, and theoretical influences. *COUNSELORS—Training of Counselor Education & Supervision*, 36(2), 144-158.

Magnuson, S., Norem, K., & Wilcoxon, A. (2000). Clinical Supervision of Prelicensed Counselors: Recommendations for Consideration and Practice. *Journal of Mental Health Counseling*, 22 (2) 176-189.

Malone, T. P., & Whitaker, C. A. (1981). *The roots of psychotherapy*. New York: Brunner/Mazel, Publishers.

Powell, G. S. *The effects of training wives in communication skills upon the marital satisfaction of both spouses*. Unpublished doctoral dissertation, University of Georgia, Athens.

Rogers, C.R. (1942). *Counseling and psychotherapy: Newer concepts in practice*. New York: Houghton Mifflin Company

Rogers, (1977). *On personal power*. New York: A Delta Book.

Rogers, C.R. (1980). *A way of being*. Boston: Houghton Mifflin Company.

Rules and Regulations for the State of Georgia. (2002). Professional Counselors Amended, 135-5.02 (a) 4.
Http://ganet.org.rules/index.cgi?base=135/5/02/.

Rules and Regulations for the State of Georgia. (2002a). Professional Counselors Amended, 135-5.02 5. Http://ganet.org.rules/index.cgi?base=135/5/02.

Wolberg, L. R. (1977). *The technique of psychotherapy* (Part 1). New York: Grune and Stratton.

0-595-29530-4